10 Ways to Future-Proof Yourself, Fearlessly Innovate, and Succeed Despite Uncertainty

# MAKE CHANGE WORK FOR YOU

SCOTT STEINBERG

I0487618

# A NEW BLUEPRINT FOR SUCCESS IN AN INCREASINGLY UNCERTAIN WORLD.

## FEATURES:

- 10 new success skills that can ignite your business, brand or career
- A revolutionary new system for future-proofing yourself in an increasingly uncertain world
- Practical, proven strategies for unleashing your creativity and innovation
- A simple, four-part formula for creating competitive advantage
- How to overcome the one thing holding most of us back from success

www.MakeChangeWorkForYou.com

# THE BUSINESS ETIQUETTE BIBLE

Modern and High-Tech Rules, Tips & Training for Working Professionals

BY

## SCOTT STEINBERG

www.AKeynoteSpeaker.com

# PREFACE

Watch carefully, and you can see business changing before your very eyes. A sales associate ignores a corporate trainer by spending time texting during a crucial development workshop, leading to the loss of vital knowledge and skills transfer... An intern's extremely loud and inappropriate ringtone sounds off while a key client visits the office, painting your business in a less professional light... An account executive responds to an irate customer in haste on the corporate social media account, leading to a wave of online backlash from thousands of incensed shoppers... A longstanding employee gets fired for posting comments critical of management on his or her personal blog. Any of these scenarios sound familiar? Thanks to the advent of new technologies and corresponding forms of communication, these situations are, sadly, becoming all too common.

Granted, each of the above examples may be extreme. But they do underscore a growing point of concern. Specifically: In a world where high-tech communication capabilities continue to grow by leaps and bounds and are becoming intrinsically interwoven into the fabric of commercial life, yet savvy personal communication skills and polished manners are becoming increasingly rare, how do we determine what's acceptable in business from the standpoint of everyday courtesy? And, for that matter, how do we delineate formal rules of propriety – let alone observe them – when the tools and technologies we utilize are constantly changing? Given the seismic impact that high-tech solutions and devices have on our interpersonal, interdepartmental and customer-facing exchanges, it's become a growingly difficult question to address – and one of paramount importance that we answer.

That's why this expert training guidebook was written: In hopes of equipping contemporary businesspeople with the tools and training they need to not only be courteous and respectful of clients and customers, but also responsible digital employers and employees. And, of course, encouraging all to not only take part in the conversation, but also actively engage in the discussion and debates that will ultimately shape tomorrow's rules of professional conduct and behavior, to the benefit of future generations. Not only is it becoming increasingly clear that there's a pressing need to provide both businesses and working professionals with the skills they need to positively integrate technology into their everyday lives. It's also becoming painfully apparent that there's a vital need to do it here and now, before a failure to maintain adequate standards of courtesy within the Internet's permanent and highly visible confines leaves a potentially lasting, pronounced and detrimental mark on their careers and legacies.

It's our sincere hope that the thorough guidelines laid out ahead will help you to inform and train future generations in the use of proper business, online and email etiquette, and provide you with the essential skills necessary to navigate the high-tech world's constantly shifting roadmap. Our intention is not to lay down iron-clad rules, rather, simply to create an initial foundation and set of parameters that today's growingly tech-savvy communities can contemplate, deliberate, implement and – most important-ly – expand and build upon. As the opening statement in what promises to be a long and fascinating discourse, we greatly look forward to hearing your thoughts on what looks to be one of the future's hottest topics, and engaging with millions more leading enterprises and professionals as they add their voices to the conversation.

# AN INTRODUCTION TO NETIQUETTE

Look down at your phone, look up at your computer, or even just glance around your office. Virtually every aspect of our lives — and nearly every interaction and workplace object contained within them — has been dramatically changed by the advent of technology. If you were just turning 18 today, brick-sized "portable" cell phones, PCs running on dial-up modems and televisions without time-shifting digital video recorders (DVRs) would have been the norm the year you were born. Today, smartphones offering constant online connectivity, tablet PCs featuring cloud computing services that place an entire desktop's worth of productivity apps in your carry-on, and professional social networks that instantly connect you with thousands of people worldwide are just a single tap away.

Technology used to tie you down, but now it frees you — or at least appears to do so, at a passing glance. But dig deeper and you'll soon discover the growing challenge that today's modern businesses, and businesspeople, are rapidly becoming all too aware of: For every new opportunity that innovative apps, gadgets and software programs introduce, they also present new wrinkles. With Twitter, Facebook and LinkedIn becoming a bigger part of everyday life, Google searches commonplace when researching new hires or prospective strategic partners, and the ability to post photos, videos and status updates online on-demand from virtually anywhere growing, there's no doubt that technology has become interwoven through every part of our personal and professional lives. But with great power comes the responsibility to be increasingly aware of the software and devices we use within the commercial world, how we utilize them, and the way in which our online and high-tech interactions impact others.

Case in point: Nowadays, it's not uncommon to witness twenty-somethings out for a business lunch who will suddenly pause their discussions mid-conversation and whip out their cell phones to check a new text message. Or, for that matter, high-powered salespeople merrily chattering away with contacts and connections while an airplane sits preparing for liftoff on the runway. Modern workdays, like the boundaries between jobs and personal time, are also increasingly blurring, given that our mobile devices are many times as powerful as yesterday's computers, and we're literally carrying our business around with us in our pockets. We're not only overwhelmed by the wealth of media options suddenly available on mobile devices, Web browsers and through broadband connections — we're increasingly struggling to comfortably incorporate them into our careers and professional interactions.

As is evident at a glance, these new high-tech problems are most reflected when it comes to modern etiquette and manners. These troubles aren't a passing issue confined solely to tech enthusiasts, either: More than a billion normal, everyday individuals (a great number of them working professionals) currently utilize Facebook, several hundred million connect via Twitter, and, according to CTIA – The Wireless Organization, there are now more cell phones than people in America. Moreover, the Radicati Group says that at least one out of every five people uses e-mail, and the Pew Institute found that the same amount have read an e-book over the past year. Just one problem: As popular as many of these forms of technology are today, they existed in very different forms two decades ago, if they existed at all. No wonder we're unsure how to handle them!

This is where the following manuscript – a comprehensive training guide to business "netiquette" (online and high-tech etiquette) – comes in. Designed to answer as many burning questions as possible, it aims to decode the rules of high-tech courtesy and behavior for a new generation of working professionals. An open-ended guide to manners in the age of persistent connectivity, social networks and streaming media, we've also connected with a slew of modern-day tech experts (our generation's equivalent of Ann Landers) to get their inside hints, tips and advice on how to comport yourself in the 21st century.

Note that given the pace at which technology moves, the endless (and endlessly evolving) variety of global and professional cultures that exist, and unique ways in which each individual interacts with high-tech tools, these proposed rules are merely a conversational starting point. Offering general guidelines and discussion points for experts and enthusiasts to discuss and debate, we hope that they'll provide positive suggestions that can help enhance both your interactions with others and the way in which you interface with technology itself. Only through ongoing and evolving dialogue between educators, employers, lawmakers, certified training professionals, professional associations and everyday individuals alike can we hope to truly define formal rules of online or high-tech conduct and digital citizenship. But in the interests of providing a starting guidepost to navigating the increasingly complex web of high-tech gadgets and services, and growingly sophisticated range of interactions and communications surrounding them, we hope you'll find it a welcome introduction.

For working professionals, we hope to demonstrate the best way to maintain professionalism and integrity within your field and/or on your chosen career path, and avoid the many unexpected but often arresting faux pas that could unexpectedly halt your journey. For businesses, organizations and employers, we seek to set initial training, education and workplace guidelines that will allow you to create a positive, safe, and enriching environment for your employees. For purposes of clarity and succinctness, we break the realm of high-tech and online etiquette down into ten core topics:

- Social Networks
- Cell Phones, Tablets, Electronics, and Mobile Devices
- Videoconferencing
- Email
- Blogs, Websites, and Online Newsgroups
- Corporate Blogging and Social Media Outreach
- Marketing, Public Relations and Social Campaigns
- Job Hunting and Careers
- Internet and Online Safety
- Instant Messaging and Chat Rooms

Each section will provide the information that you or your business needs to know in order to adroitly handle yourself in everyday situations. As an added bonus, we've also sprinkled in interviews and insights with leading etiquette experts, relevant discussion points of interest, and (for all you newcomers) definitions of common tech lingo. Future editions will expand and update upon the subjects contained herein. We invite you to submit your own insights, tips and suggestions at www.AKeynoteSpeaker.com – only with your help and insight can we hope to keep future generations ahead of the curve.

# SOCIAL NETWORKS

Social networks – self-contained online forums where users can share their lives and careers and engage in ongoing dialogue with others in the form of text, photos, videos, comments and other forms of high-tech communication – have grown by leaps and bounds over the past decade. More than a billion people worldwide now regularly participate in social networks, and a good portion of that participation is for business purposes.

In fact, it's fair to say that today we're juggling two business agendas: Real and virtual. However you use these networks, though, it's worth remembering that they've had a fundamental impact on how we interact with others. Before Facebook and similar sites became ubiquitous, the word "friend" referred to someone with whom we shared positive interactions and interests in real-life face-to-face settings – among them coworkers, colleagues, peers and professional acquaintances. Today, Oxford Dictionaries' suite of products actually includes the following definition for the term: "A contact on a social networking website." When we call someone a "friend," we now distinguish between a social network acquaintance and an actual friend – in the latter case, someone we've met in real life and may even enjoy a deeper personal connection with.

Key to remember here: A friend or, in this case, a professional associate on Facebook, Twitter, or other social networks may not be someone we've spent time with in the real world, or know particularly well. But they may not be complete strangers, either – or even someone in-between. This begs the question: What do you share with business associates you've never connected with in everyday life, know next to nothing about, or perhaps have just exchanged minor pleasantries in passing? We all have to be careful sharing information amongst today's fluid social circle. Doubly so, since more unscrupulous individuals could use information against us and our companies, or share sensitive data with other people that we wouldn't trust at all.

Another issue that social networks present is the false sense of security they convey – much like the Internet itself. From our perspective, we're staring at a cold, inanimate PC monitor, faceless webcam, or glossy smartphone screen, making it easy to forget that literally billions of people – including colleagues, employees, bosses and potential customers or partners – may be staring back. And, for that matter, can conceivably access anything we post online, which may live on via the Internet forever. Even top celebrities, who of all people should know how public their lives are, have made epic mistakes, tweeting offensive jokes, posting risqué photos, and even slandering other people, simply because they didn't remember the number one rule of the Internet: Don't post something you'd be ashamed to share with the public at large.

Also crucial to keep in mind when entering the social networking world, given its high level of visibility and shared nature: One should always avoid discussing topics that act as lightning rods in everyday social situations. Think of your time in the social network realm as similar to that spent at a formal business cocktail party: Politics, religion, sex, and other potentially controversial subjects are typically best left off the table. While it is ultimately up to you what you choose to share, and acceptance levels differ by individual audience, it always pays to remember the following maxim: Using a social network automatically means that you are in shared, and oftentimes mixed, company — and what appears to be a safe, cut-and-dried subject (professional or otherwise) to you may seem like a radical, offensive idea to others online.

# LEADING SERVICES

Following is a breakdown of five major networks, including LinkedIn, Facebook, Twitter, Pinterest and Google+, each with a summary, pros and cons, and insider tips to help make your experiences on them both safe and fulfilling.

## LinkedIn

The largest professional social network, LinkedIn focuses on connecting you with co-workers, employers, and colleagues. It also allows you to create a virtual résumé and tear sheet of testimonials that can be shared with potential employers, and reach out to potential peers and mentors.

**Benefits:**
- Great way to stay connected with colleagues and/or source testimonials even after a job ends
- Avoids the personal, mundane information plaguing other sites in favor of strictly professional communications
- Can connect you to new job opportunities and individuals through mutual introductions

**Challenges:**
- Users don't always update their profile, so information may not be current, or relevant to present jobs and skill sets

- You may find yourself fielding inappropriate or unwanted requests for connections, introductions, or recommendations from third parties, known or otherwise
- Extended site features and connection options require a paid annual professional membership fee

**Inside Tips:**
- Use a real-life headshot of yourself as your profile photo, not cartoon avatars, product shots or random images: It's imperative to convey a professional image.
- Only ask for testimonials from people that you've intimately worked with in the past.
- Be honest when providing your online résumé, as former and present colleagues are likely on LinkedIn, too. Likewise, multiple copies of one's résumé may readily be available online – be careful that these documents don't contradict.
- When attempting to connect with strangers, at a bare minimum, fill out the contact section and explain who you are and why you'd like to sync up with them.
- Give connected colleagues a heads-up to confirm their approval before introducing or connecting them to another person in your network.
- Reaching out to pitch contacts via LinkedIn and/or blasting out promotional or news announcements through the service en masse is frowned upon – as a general rule, any such outreach should be made through alternate channels, e.g. direct work email addresses.

# Facebook

Enjoyed by hundreds of millions of users, Facebook allows you to share thoughts (in the form of text posts called status updates), pictures, and video with other real-life individuals connected to the service (called friends). Note that while Facebook posts can be limited to certain groups, the majority of interactions are public, and highly

**When Is the Best Time to Connect On LinkedIn?**

"I think any time is appropriate to connect on LinkedIn. If you're looking to connect with someone you don't know, but want to get to know professionally, make your agenda known when you first make initial contact. Don't send the generic "I'd like to add you to my network" email, but instead clarify who you are, why you're reaching out and why you think it's important to connect."

-Jeana Lee Tahnk, www.jeanatahnk.com, Tech Writer and PR Consultant visible. Facebook's widespread popularity, near ubiquity on set-top and mobile devices, and visibly social nature, as well as easy comment and response system, make it popular with businesses looking to quickly engage sizable communities.

**Benefits:**
- Free and easy to use, and accessible from many major high-tech devices
- Extremely popular – many people, business and brands you'll know are on it, and may be amenable to using the service to connect
- Fast and simple sharing of text and multimedia content with others

**Challenges:**
- Ever-changing set of privacy settings and features, which may prove challenging to keep up with
- Some may find it difficult and time-consuming to share content specifically curated to be safe for professional consumption with specific groups or subsets of friends
- Posting frequency must be carefully considered: Tempting as it may be to constantly promote, users' news feeds and notifications can get quickly become clogged, leading to negative responses and reactions.

**Inside Tips:**
- Be careful "Liking" a negative or controversial status update, as it may alienate people and, depending on their status, even offend the person who posted it. Note that doing so may also cause viewers to take it as a sign of your tacit approval or endorsement.
- Realize that there may be consequences to linking Twitter to your Facebook account, as it may spam others' feeds by repeatedly posting throughout the day.
- Add a personalized and professional note when you ask to be someone's friend on Facebook explaining who you are and why you want to be friends, unless you happen to know the person well in real life.
- Do not feel obligated to friend someone back, especially individuals you don't know, since that may give them access to personal information about you.
- Adjust your settings so you have control over who posts on your wall, tags you in pictures and – via status updates or other methods – can reveal where you are located.
- Always log or sign out of your Facebook account when done using it – especially on shared devices.

**Personal Versus Professional Usage:**

• If you plan on using Facebook to promote yourself professionally, you may want to have two accounts — one with your actual name for professional purposes and one with a personal nickname for just friends and family, especially if your friends and family members may post things that your employer, employees or clients might object to.

• Note that contacts may use the service primarily for personal purposes, and not take kindly to business postings: Having a separate business account or page in addition to your personal account is often advisable, and can be a highly effective way to promote your business that offers great exposure and opportunities to attract new customers or clients.

• Make sure you understand privacy settings so that you have control over who sees timeline posts, tags, photos and other postings.

• You may wish to assign one key social media-savvy person to be responsible for business accounts, whose responsibilities include curating and editing content to ensure that all posts and links are consistent and clearly representative of your business, branding and corporate image.

## Twitter

Twitter is a social or 'micro-blogging' network that lets you share short statements (called "tweets") in the form of text updates that clock in at 140 characters or less. As with Facebook, you can follow people on Twitter and be followed by others, allowing users to track your activity and status updates. Interesting tweets can also be shared (retweeted) with your own friends and followers. Many businesses and global corporations use Twitter as a way to share news or deals, or spark interest in varied topics and announcements, as its ease of use and availability on a myriad of devices make it a simple and efficient way for information and dialogue to spread.

**Benefits:**

• Free of charge, Twitter offers a handy way to exchange short messages, deals or news updates suitable for brief browsing sessions and accessible from most major high-tech devices

• Fast way to find out what's trending in the world at large, and share information or interesting tidbits at record speed.

• Lets you quickly connect with and follow the activity of colleagues, friends and strangers alike

**Challenges:**

- Even private information can be easily shared by strangers in seconds, and impulse-driven nature may lead to unwise posts and responses
- Rapid post and response system can lead to high incidence rates, and communications cycles take place at a much more accelerated pace than corporations are typically used to
- Short nature of messages doesn't lend itself well to deep conversations or conveying emotional nuance, and clarity, depth and subtle details are often sacrificed for brevity's sake

**Inside Tips:**

- When in doubt about balancing informational and promotional efforts, use the 80-20 rule of thumb: Use your tweets to promote interesting information and content others have created 80 percent of the time, then 20 percent to promote yourself or your business professionally.
- With regard to interpersonal communications, while you cannot directly retweet tweets from private accounts, it's important to avoid copying and pasting them, too, as private tweets have been made classified for a reason.
- It is not required for you to follow people, businesses or brands who have chosen to follow you (although doing so in return can be seen as a polite gesture). However, it is important to acknowledge them when they reply to or retweet one of your public messages: Online dialogue works two ways.
- Think before you post: Is the item you're planning to share of interest and relevant to those who follow you? And how can you phrase or present it in such a way to offer them maximum value while minimizing self-promotional overtones?
- Be careful not only what you post, but also when posting links to pictures, videos, and websites that may be unsuitable for viewing at work.
- As noted in the book Damon Brown's Simple Guide to Twitter, retweeting a post gives the impression that you agree with it, as no additional context is provided – be careful what you or your business inadvertently endorse.
- Given Twitter's constant connectivity and often rapid-response nature, always pause and reconsider posts before you tweet – once publicly made, statements cannot be taken back.

**Personal Versus Professional Usage:**

- If you plan on using Twitter to promote yourself or your business professionally, you may wish to have two accounts – one with your actual or trade name for professional purposes, and one with a personal nickname for just friends and family to keep the personal and professional separate.

- Create a dedicated business account can be a great way to promote your brand, separate personal from professional opinions, and provide great exposure, helping you attract or maintain customers and clients by providing content with a professional bent that personal contacts may be less inclined to enjoy receiving notices about or links to.
- As with postings on other social networks, you may wish to assign one key social media-savvy person to be responsible for business accounts, whose responsibilities include curating and editing content to ensure that all posts and links are consistent and clearly representative of your business' online image and branding.

## Pinterest

This visually stunning social network allows you to post gorgeous photos, pictures, recipes, articles and more online. Essentially a virtual pinboard on which ideas and artwork can be shared, it presents a highly graphical way to share business or personal interests, and create catalogue-style product presentations. The platform works best for companies or professionals looking to showcase striking and visually-inclined information, e.g. a snapshot of new offerings, career portfolios and retrospectives, or photos from recent meetings and events.

**Benefits:**
- Great way to stay connected with colleagues and customers, especially if your business or brand is easily communicable through visual mediums
- Provides a wonderful way to promote anything (products, events, showroom demos, etc.) that lends itself well to photography
- Offers a great opportunity to create value for customers and connect with a broader audience, who can quickly view and enjoy information shared

**Challenges:**
- Maintaining audience interest may require more frequent updates, sharing and upkeep than on other social networks
- Less effective for visually nondescript items or promotions that cannot be easily communicated at a glance
- Through growing by leaps and bounds in popularity, enjoys less of a following, and less ubiquity, than Facebook or Twitter

**Inside Tips:**
- Tempting as it may be to share offbeat or unique photos, remember to use only images that best represent yourself or your business in a manner that suits your

professional personality. It's imperative to convey a professional image that's in line with your image and brand.

- Always promote colleagues' and employees' work where appropriate, and be gracious about shining the spotlight on peers', partners' and third parties as well – a lesson equally applicable to other social networks as well.
- Look for ways to create value with viewers: Rather than simply posting shots of your bakery's latest creations, for example, you might also share seasonal recipes, photos highlighting loyal customers, or images illustrating how donations that shoppers make on-location are used to help members of the local community.

## Google+

Newer than the other social networks, Google+ adopts an approach similar to Facebook's, but offers the option to divide contacts into circles – unique groups whose access to specific information you can control. Essentially, users can individually segment groups by relation, topic or category (e.g. colleagues, golfing buddies, personal friends, etc.), then comment on statuses and share items amongst specific circles to control the flow of information. Because it allows for greater control of information flow, it also presents the opportunity to maintain better separation of personal and professional topics.

**Benefits:**
- Easy to post multimedia from all Google services, including YouTube, to your profile and share with contacts, and enjoy high-quality group chat options
- The +1 system and supporting buttons lets you quickly and easily share interesting items from all across the web, including business news or articles and expert insights
- Friends can be subdivided into private circles (work, school, personal acquaintances, family, etc.) so you can control whom content is shared with, and to what extent

**Challenges:**
- May be less widely utilized by contacts and acquaintances than other social networks mentioned here
- Despite precautions, it's still easy to unintentionally share private or unwanted information with the wrong circle
- Still working to differentiate itself from rivals, and may be seen as less intuitive for beginners than visually-oriented competitors such as Pinterest

**Inside Tips:**

• As with Facebook, use caution when approving (giving a +1) to a negative or controversial status update – this may be seen as an endorsement of its contents.

• Carefully craft your circles so you'll share notes only with appropriate parties – this allows you to avoid inadvertently sharing data with unreceptive or inappropriate audiences.

• As of recent reports, Google ties your actions together across all its services, so be aware that it can now track your activities from Google+ to YouTube to Google Maps.

• Do not automatically reciprocate adding a contact to your circle until you are sure that you know them or want to be connected to them – and then be careful which circle you add them to.

• For your protection, when not in use, log out of your Google+ account on your phone just as you would on your home or laptop computer.

# SOCIAL NETWORKING TIPS

## What's OK to Share?

• Sharing extremely-opinionated viewpoints (e.g. political leanings or thoughts on controversial topics of all kinds) can be a lightning rod online. Think twice before liking supporting status updates or posting such opinions, which can incite and aggravate others (and live on in perpetuity). If you feel the need to express these opinions, consider confining such communications to private exchanges with individual friends, or specific Facebook or Google+ groups. Ultimately though, it's important to remember: If you don't have anything nice to say, perhaps it's best left unsaid – a point doubly worth noting, as even private

## A BETTER APPROACH TO SOCIAL NETWORKING

Think you've got social network etiquette mastered? KTLA-TV Los Angeles tech reporter Rich DeMuro (@RichDeMuro) says it never hurts to think twice before hitting send. Below are his thoughts on how to be a more polite and respectful social media user:

1. Don't be an over-sharer. People will appreciate well-curated shares more than you passing along every single article that you've stumbled across. The better you are about sharing, the more people will look forward to what you post, instead of routinely skipping over your posts.

2. My big pet peeve when it comes to social media is people sharing "big" links. I call big links anything that comes from a major blog or site that pretty much everyone checks on a daily basis. If you must share, at least bring something new to the conversation like your opinion or analysis of the topic.

3. Checking in has become very popular online, and the practice has its place. For

example: I find it handy to check in at places where I want other people to know I'm there, such as a conference or event. Just watch the auto-posts of all those badges on the various social networks. You'd be surprised how many people don't care that you just unlocked a "swarm."

4. Watch what you upload and who you tag. In the end, it's really up to the end user to filter out what they want their followers to see... but use a little good judgment when you're uploading pictures and tagging your colleagues. Make good use of Facebook's friend lists feature to target your sharing and narrow down the potential exposure.

5. Don't mistakenly share sensitive info. Many people don't realize that photos and tweets can contain geo-tags that can pinpoint your location down to a few feet. If you don't want everyone in the world to know exactly where you are posting from, turn these GPS features off.

communications can inadvertently and easily become public online.

• Posting embarrassing, revealing or unprofessional photos of yourself or business colleagues should be avoided at all costs. Remember: Images you share may be taken at face value, and/or viewed as representative of your character – not to mention live on forever on the Internet. What seems cute at the office party or during the off-hours may not seem quite so endearing to current or future customers or employers.

• Never post photos of others, including customers, without their express permission.

• Relationship or personal drama is best kept private. If you don't want your employer or employees to know, don't post it at all.

• As a rule of thumb, uncomfortable or revealing personal information, i.e. details of you or your family's struggles with psychological or health-related issues, should be shared sparingly, if at all, and only in the latter case if there is a legitimately pressing business reason that others need to know this information. Note that content shared online may further be available for public viewing, and inadvertently expose you or your family to potential risk and/or embarrassment.

• To minimize risks of crime, vandalism or identity theft, never share intimate personal details including birthdates, phone numbers, addresses, schools or hometowns online. Never let others know when you'll be away from your business, especially for any given length of time, e.g. while on vacation.

• Avoid posting on social networks unless you have a tight grasp over your privacy settings, and are completely comfortable with the group of online friends and contacts that your updates will be shared with.

## Tone of Voice and Attitude

• Professionalism is imperative – if you wouldn't say it in a workplace or professional setting, don't say it online, in the most public of forums.
• Politeness and respect are vital: Always be considerate of others, and treat them the way that you'd wish to be treated.
• Avoid bad-mouthing the competition or other users as it will negatively impact your image and colleagues or clients may judge you based on these actions.
• Maintain a positive tone and attitude: Negativity, complaints and condescending messages often reflect poorly on the poster.
• Bragging and self-aggrandizing statements should be avoided, and making them may cause you to lose followers.
• Since social networks are shared venues enjoyed in mixed company, always avoid using vulgar language and making derogatory remarks.
• Demanding that others share your status updates, projects, thoughts or ideas is inappropriate.
• Reserve confidential discussions for private message threads or, better yet, phone calls, emails or other venues where interactions aren't recorded in perpetuity online.
• Be advised that conversational nuances and subtle shifts in tone or personality may be lost in translation, and that individual users may interpret messages differently: Consider how posts will be read and interpreted before sending.
• Poor spelling, punctuation, grammar and choice of words can reflect equally poorly upon the individual or business – proofread all communications before sending. Shorthand, abbreviations and online slang should be avoided if possible, and used only in the most informal of conversations.

## Being a Responsible User

• Understand that each social network has its own rules of conduct, social norms and methods of interaction. Before utilizing one, take a moment to step back and observe how interactions take place, so you can discern appropriate rules of posting, sharing and behavior.
• Assume that everything you post online can be seen by others, as even major social networks have suffered privacy breaches.
• Do not share information that online friends have shared with you in confidence, i.e. quoting someone's private tweet to you.
• Log out of all your social networks when finished using them, or when you are using a computer or mobile device that isn't yours.

- Realize that everything posted online lives on the Internet permanently, and may be available for public viewing.
- Never forget: Despite their seemingly intimacy, social networks are among the most public of spaces – it's important to conduct yourself on them as you would in any shared setting.
- You reserve the exclusive right, and it is wholly appropriate, to decline friend requests from strangers or users you don't feel will contribute to the atmosphere of positive, professional and open dialogue on your business' public forums.
- Privacy and personal comfort are paramount: At no point should you feel compelled to respond to messages or queries from people you don't know.
- Before posting on others' profiles or walls, or tagging them in your own posts, consider how your actions and/or statements may be perceived, and if they may potentially cast them in a negative light and/or embarrass them.
- Use privacy settings to limit who can view your posts and shares.
- When asking someone you don't know to be your friend, send a short message explaining who you are and why you're attempting to contact them.

## Juggling Personal vs. Professional Interactions

**Friending and De-Friending Others, Including Real-Life Friends and Family**
- Only friend people you would be comfortable sharing the ins-and-outs of your day (including both off-hours time and the professional workday) with in real life.
- It is OK to de-friend any and all individuals whom you don't feel comfortable sharing updates with. Many sites allow you to quietly de-friend individuals without notifying them, or ignore friend requests in perpetuity, while allowing the option for them to continue receiving status updates.
- If you're not ready to de-friend a contact completely on a social network, consider moving them into a lower-profile friend category where you can share fewer posts with them and receive less information about their lives.
- In many cases, there is no notice sent when you de-friend a person, so they won't know they've been downgraded unless they happen to visit your page and don't see the respective friend icon checked.

**When to Log Off**
- Always log off after using public computers or high-tech devices.
- Never click the "Remember Me" or "Remember My Password" option when logging into a social network unless you own the device from which it's being accessed, as others may be able to access your social network in your absence.
- Should a coworker, colleague or other user inadvertently leave their login open,

under no circumstance is it appropriate to utilize or sift through their personal accounts.

## Adding Photos
• Facebook, Twitter, LinkedIn, and Google+ all have policies against profane or violent photos – none of which are appropriate to share.
• A picture is worth a thousand words – make sure they're all positive: As a general rule, only post photos that you would be comfortable sharing with your coworkers, strategic partners and clients.
• Be careful tagging others in photos, as they may not wish the photo or its contents to be visible to others on the site.
• Never, ever post risqué or potentially controversial photos if you don't want your boss, colleagues or employees to see them. Even better: Don't post them at all.

## Think Before You Post
• Think carefully before posting on someone's wall or adding people to groups, and always seek their permission in advance.
• Context is everything as well: Be sure to consider the ramifications of making these connections in advance, as some users may be annoyed or insulted that you think they are interested in certain publicly-visible topics or brands.
• Before you post, reconsider. Posting an inappropriate message or piece of content on someone's wall can get them in trouble with their employers, colleagues or clients. When in doubt, consider sending a private message or email with the link instead.

## Commenting on Posts
• Cursing, incendiary and salacious language is inappropriate to post under any circumstance.
• Always avoid being judgmental of others' opinions.
• Realize that certain comments (intimate missives, items relating to personal or family issues, etc.) are best reserved for a phone call, sympathy card, or personal gesture.
• Be advised that commentary may be misconstrued or taken out of context – always consider the way in which you may be perceived.
• Understand that someone is always watching. Even courts of law can now subpoena tweets or Facebook posts. While you may be joking in real-life, even the most sarcastic statements can potentially seem damning when taken out of context – you never know what may come back to haunt you or your business.
• Re-Read your posts. Many of us depend on auto-fill features when entering our messages online, but if you don't read what you've written, you may be surprised by typos and instances where the entirely wrong word (world...) was entered.

## SHOULD YOU BEFRIEND YOUR BOSS ONLINE?

Michael Dsupin, CEO of the IT staffing agency The Talener Group (www.talener.com), knows how important the relationship between supervisor and employee can be — and the dynamics that go into it. This is what he had to say about accepting a Facebook friend request from your boss:

"If this happened five years earlier, I probably wouldn't think anything of it and harmlessly accept my supervisor's friend request. Now that the topic has become such a lightning rod, if I were approached by my boss I would have to politely say no. One thing that I have learned in my 16 years of business is not to let a problem sit there unattended. The longer left unaddressed, the hotter the topic. So immediately upon receiving a friend request from a supervisor, co-worker or manager, I would deny the friend request. And then, before leaving for the day, I would pull that person aside and say to them, "I appreciate your friend request, however I have a lot of personal pictures on my profile from my childhood and adolescence

## Work-Specific Social Network Tips

### Accessing Social Networks at Work
- Check your employer's work policy, as frequenting certain social networks during on-the-job hours may be inappropriate or even grounds for dismissal.
- While attitudes towards social networks may differ depending on your position, it's safe to assume that spending time on social networks is frowned upon during work hours.
- Your favorite social network app or video game may tell everyone when you're fiddling with it during work hours, so avoid doing it when you should be otherwise professionally occupied.

### Connecting with Co-Workers and Bosses
- Before connecting with your boss or employees on social networks, consider if you'd still want to be connected to them if they weren't your coworkers, i.e. if you ever leave the position.
- Prior to requesting or accepting connections from colleagues, think about material you're apt to share — is it appropriate for their consumption?
- Note that connecting with colleagues and supervisors may expose you or them to information and influences that may make either party uncomfortable — be certain to understand the risk you're taking in doing so.
- When posting status updates, photos or videos, or interacting online, let professionalism rule: If it's unsafe to say or share at the office, it's not something you should project online.
- Use caution when connecting with co-workers, as more unscrupulous colleagues could use private information obtained from social networks against you.
- If you do wish to connect with co-workers, LinkedIn is a good professional choice. Chances

are, your bosses and even some of your colleagues, have already checked out your LinkedIn profile.

## Managing Photos and Videos

• Do not tag coworkers without their permission. Likewise, do not tag colleagues in images and videos that may be perceived as unprofessional, inappropriate or controversial, even within private social networks – and, for judgment's sake, always err on the side of extreme caution.

• Set social networks to send you an alert whenever you are tagged in a photo or video, and check such postings immediately to make sure you are comfortable with the content and context contained within.

• While individual preference may differ here, it's best to save yourself some trouble and skip posting content from informal work gatherings, i.e. office party photos or videos from corporate getaways, entirely. Such settings seldom lend themselves to depictions consistent with one's professional or corporate image, and not all may be comfortable with the manner in which they're portrayed in media captured at these events.

## What's Not OK to Post

• Avoid voicing strong political, religious or social views on networks you share with customers, colleagues and bosses. If it's not OK to say at work, it's not OK to post on the Internet.

• Do not post negative, controversial, rude or potentially insulting commentary in online spaces.

• Don't speak ill of others, or publicly deride competitors – there's something to be said for good sportsmanship.

• Keep discussions about office politics off all social networks and online spaces, even those that you consider to be private.

that don't accurately reflect the person that I am today. I'd hate to tarnish my image or reputation within the firm based upon some old photos posted by my close friends or family. I hope you understand."

By nipping it in the bud immediately, the topic is a moot point, and you can go about your business regularly tomorrow, knowing that it is covered. "

## THE RULES OF ONLINE BEHAVIOR

When it comes to managing online interactions, New York City-based tech and lifestyle writer Erica Swallow (http://www.ericaswallow.com) knows her stuff. The owner of Southern Swallow Productions and director of community at Contently, Swallow took time out to explain the perils of social networking with coworkers, the art of commenting constructively on blogs, and how not to aggravate others with your high-tech interactions.

**Q:** What is the most common social gaffe people make when using their cell phone?

**A:** Because we rely on our cell phones so much these days, there are tons of ways to find yourself in sticky social situations, but people are increasingly more forgiving when you do. The worst social gaffe people make with their cell phones is to let them ring [in public]. I'm a firm believer that cell phones should stay on vibrate. There is no reason unless your spouse is in labor or you have a family member in the hospital to have the ringer or ringtone on. Other social faux pas regarding the cell

• It is wholly inappropriate to use social networks to air dirty laundry, or speak negatively of former, current or prospective employers or colleagues.

### Ways to Keep it Professional

• Respond respectfully to commentary aimed at you, or do not respond at all.
• Decide how you want to use a social network (for work, social, or personal purposes, or some combination thereof) before you join and begin inviting others to it. Let this decision guide the type of content posted and tone of voice you adopt.
• Promote others more than you promote yourself to avoid looking selfish (and build good karma).
• Be supportive of others and treat them with the same care and dignity you'd ask for yourself.

## Ways to Use Social Networks to Your Professional Advantage

### Smart Online Career Building

• Keep all online profile pictures professional and reflective of the same respectful image that you project on the job.
• All online postings and presences may be accessible to recruiters, colleagues, strategic partners or clients: As such, it's essential to post and represent both yourself and your business at all times with the utmost integrity and professionalism — like the saying goes, everyone's a brand ambassador.
• Know that anything you say, post and promote online can and will be publicly scrutinized, and/or possibly taken out of context — make certain you put your best foot forward when you use social networks, and think about how your words and actions may be interpreted, whether made in jest or otherwise.
• Separate professional and personal expressions

online. (See below for more tips.)

• Make certain that your professional history, as viewed in resumes and online profiles, is consistent. Recruiters will immediately be suspicious of any applicant where obvious discrepancies exist, especially where they may suggest padding or false statements.

## Separating Public from Private

• Utilize differing profiles or groups of contacts when posting material to ensure that you're separating information for consumption by personal contacts from professional. When you have these disparate groups lumped together into one giant "friends" list, it's all too easy to accidentally post inappropriate, incorrect or ill-advised messages or updates where they can be seen by the wrong audience, to your detriment.

• Consider content, tone of voice and nature of updates when posting them to social networks, and whether material would be considered suitable for use in professional exchanges, or reflect positively upon you in a career-related context, prior to hitting send. While you may enjoy a casual relationship with clients, sharing information about off-hours activities and personal hobbies may fall under the category of TMI (too much information).

• When in doubt, err on the side of caution: Any material you'd think twice about mentioning or sharing at the office shouldn't be shared online for sake of safety and propriety — you can never be too careful.

## Pitching Through Social Networks

• With rare exceptions, if someone wanted to hear your pitch, you would already have his or her email address — contacting them out of the blue on social networks is inappropriate.

phone include texting or talking during performances or movies, making calls while on public transit or in crowded places, and playing games or music aloud (without earphones) while others are around.

**Q:** Any suggestions you can offer for more appropriate commenting when conversing on blogs?

**A:** Blog comments are most interesting when they are insightful, but brief compliments are also welcome. No matter how long, blog comments should be interesting and add to the conversation, however. Length doesn't really matter, as long as your comment is interesting. I've seen commenters practically write entire blog posts of their own in the comments section, and I've been completely enthralled. In this case, the reader usually comments on the writer's work and add his or her own thoughts and opinions on the matter. Meanwhile, I also see a lot of short, congratulatory messages posted such as "nicely written" and "cool examples," and those are just as welcome, though not as original and definitely not thought-provoking.

**Q:** From a business standpoint, how do you handle your supervisor wanting to be friends on Facebook?

**A:** There are three options here: Accept, decline or leave your supervisor in purgatory. I prefer to either accept or leave people in purgatory, no matter who they are. After all, I feel it's really not my place to "decline" or "reject" a friendship. I am flattered when someone is interested enough to "friend" me on Facebook, but I follow the "must have met a few times [in real-life]" rule before adding people.

When it comes to supervisors, I am happy to add them. "Work" and "life" are not separate entities for me – I live, and while living, I have work, and I have free time. I am an equal-opportunity friend, accepting workmates as well as playmates. I recommend that others think about life in a similar way – it's much more organic. And furthermore, if a supervisor can't accept you for you, including every bit of Facebook information you've amassed over the years, maybe they aren't deserving of your service.

If, however, you do not want to be friends with your supervisor,

• Under no circumstances should you pitch an idea, product, or job opportunity on someone's public wall or profile.
• Some users provide professional contact information on their public profile – using it may be acceptable in some cases, though reaching out via any personal addresses contained therein (janedoe@gmail.com) is not.

### Engaging in Online Exchanges

• It's perfectly respectful (and expected) that you will want to follow influencers, companies and colleagues in your chosen career path or industry. As a sign of respect, make a point of both conversing with them, adding your thoughts to dialogue they've begun, and passing along updates they've shared with resonate to others who might enjoy them.
• Subscribe to RSS feeds that will update you on what is most important in your industry or business, then consider retweeting or reposting where appropriate and adding your own insights to provide maximum benefit for your own readers or viewers.
• Observe and follow those with whom you'd like to do business: Many times, they'll ask questions or request suggestions or input – at these times, you might consider crafting appropriate (i.e. not overly self-promotional) responses, tweets, posts, etc. that can help them meet these needs while creating win-win scenarios with positive outcomes for you as well.
• When posting and sharing updates, be sure to promote others more than yourself – do so, and you'll make friends, gain more followers, and ultimately invite others to wish to respond in kind.
• When you are looking for a job, it's OK to gently let the world know with a status update or two here and there that you're "seeking new

opportunities" – however, doing so repeatedly, forcefully and/or over extended periods of time can come across as off-putting. Always consider how such updates might be received, appropriate posting frequencies, and always be positive and upbeat in tone: Anger, sadness and desperation seldom translate well, online or otherwise.

simply declining their invite will do. You don't have to explain, but if he or she asks, you can just say that you only add close friends to your Facebook account. Or, if purgatory sounds more appealing, just leave your boss waiting for an answer... forever.

# CELL PHONES, TABLETS, ELECTRONICS & MOBILE DEVICES

Mobile devices have truly taken off over the past few years, and more than ever, businesses are electronically connected and wired. Amazingly, in 2011, CTIA found that there were now more cell phones (about 328 million) than people (about 315 million) in the US, and some people even have two phones, one for personal and one for business! The average smartphone allows employees to access email, text colleagues, download documents, research projects, take and share photos, conduct virtual meetings and more. As a result, maintaining proper mobile etiquette for business is more important than ever.

## General Tips

### When to Use Phones and Mobile Devices

• Devices should be turned off during meetings, presentations, training sessions, meals, and conversations. They should also be shut down when entering conferences, restaurants, and religious institutions, or attending professional functions. As a rule of thumb, devices should be put away and silenced at any time they might disturb others, i.e. when in shared company.

• If you must keep your phone on because you're expecting an important message or communication, silence it or set the ringer to vibrate. Under optimal scenarios, calls will be forwarded to voicemail, where you can listen and respond to them later.

• If you cannot avoid having to take a call or text, politely excuse yourself from the scenario or discussion, as you would when going to the bathroom.

• Whether in public or private spaces, always keep conversation levels to a respectful volume. Shouting into your phone is inappropriate.

• If unavoidable, calls made in public should be kept as short, sweet and quiet as possible, and confined to crowded or noisier areas where less private space is anticipated.

• Note that should you choose to interrupt exchanges to take calls, the longer you keep other parties waiting, the greater their potential annoyance.

• When speaking in public spaces, avoid sharing private information, as it may be overhead and subsequently shared with others.

• Do not turn phones on during public performances, business meetings, and other shared moments that could disturb individuals or large groups of people.

• Phones should not be used in enclosed spaces such as elevators, restaurants and other places where your conversations may intrude upon or annoy others. If you need to make a call, politely excuse yourself and step outside to do so, or wait until you're in a less private or intrusive setting.

- If placed on vibrate, note that phones should be stored in a purse or pocket, so as not to make noise when they shake against a hard surface, e.g. the dinner table, disturbing others with the sound of their vibrations.
- Ringtones may add character to incoming calls, but consider the message they send: Clients may not equate Justin Bieber's falsetto with something they'd expect to hear emanating from the suit pocket of a serious professional.
- Texting or talking on your cell phone while driving may distract you, impair reaction times and endanger others, and should therefore be avoided at all costs. Hands-free wireless Bluetooth headsets may mitigate some issues, but the best solution is to pull over, park and finish conversations before resuming travel.

### Everyday Advice and Hints

- Turn off phones' displays when not in use to avoid accidentally dialing contacts.
- Shut down phones and other high-tech devices while in darkened conventional halls or meeting spaces, and don't use them during such low-light scenarios – screens may light up and detract from fellow attendees' enjoyment.
- Take caution when choosing contacts to email or dial – an accidental slip of the finger, or gaffe made by built-in auto-correction features, may result in your contacting the wrong party.
- Be courteous and timely about responding to calls, emails and texts – if it takes you longer than 24 hours to get back to the sender, you may want to send a brief note with an ETA when a proper response can be expected. ("Sincerest apologies, I've been busy at work, but I'll do my best to get back to you within the next day or so.")
- Should you accidentally receive a call or text intended for someone else, a simple "sorry, wrong number" will suffice to prevent further communication. Resist the temptation to be rude, snarky or annoyed when responding, and realize that ignoring the missive may result in subsequent attempts at communication.
- Bluetooth wireless earpieces and headsets should always be turned off and taken out when not in use, and are inappropriate to use while conversing with other. Similarly, they should not be used in enclosed spaces, where they may disturb others. Limited use in high-traffic or noisy public spaces may be acceptable – the same rules for using cell phones, as presented in When to Use Phones and Mobile Devices, apply.

### Cameras and Video Cameras

- Do not photograph or record videos of others without their knowledge and permission.
- Do not take pictures or videos that would offend or embarrass subjects.

- Do not share and post snapshots or film clips of others without their approval.
- Do not use cameras and camcorders in private or intimate spaces including bathrooms, showers, locker rooms, dressing rooms or other spaces where doing so may violate personal privacy and/or the law.
- Do not use cameras and video cameras in houses of worship, during intimate personal or family occasions, or in group or shared settings that may jeopardize others' privacy (i.e. wherever the expectation of privacy is enjoyed) or the privacy of their children (ex: your local daycare).

**Texting and Messaging**
- When abbreviating messages, show knowledge and respect of how the other party may interpret these communications – texts sent to your boss should look differently than texts sent to a 20-something customer, as each will comprehend and react to messages differently.
- Avoid texting private, embarrassing, intimate or confidential details, as these messages aren't just inappropriate to send – they're also all too easy to forward on and into the hands of unwanted parties.
- Note that slang, jargon, grammatical errors, and misspellings may save time and give messages a hint of character, but may reflect poorly upon you or send the wrong message about your personal communication skills. (One point, as alluded to above, is that much depends on the culture of the business you're operating in. If you're working at a cutting-edge technology startup, for instance, you might certainly have more latitude than, say, if you worked in a more traditionally conservative organization such as a bank or brokerage firm.)
- As with emails or any form of written high-tech communication, note that tone or intention may be hard to convey through texting, and messages may be perceived incorrectly or taken out of context. Consider before sending if the information is best conveyed with a phone call, short note or alternate form of communication.
- Double check names and numbers before texting, especially if making a confidential statement, lest you risk accidentally reach out to the wrong party.
- Show courtesy for others' time, patience and phone bill by switching from group texts to reaching out to individuals via direct texts when the conversation becomes irrelevant to others, and ask that they reciprocate.
- Don't send others text messages without asking first – not all subscribe to ongoing texting plans, and recipients may incur billing charges as a result.
- Text messaging is strictly casual in nature, and inappropriate for weightier or more meaningful communications. For more important news or interactions (ending a professional relationship, sharing unfortunate events, etc.) a phone call or in-person exchange is more appropriate.

- Texts should be kept brief – if you need to say more than can be fit into a few lines, write an email or pick up the phone instead.
- Avoid smiley faces, frowny faces or other imagery where possible, unless you enjoy a relaxed working relationship with the other party being communicated with, to avoid the appearance of unprofessionalism – such expressions are much more geared towards the exchange of casual and informal conversation.
- Be respectful of others and don't carpet bomb them with texts – before sending, consider if they really need to receive your commentary in parts from the main body of the message.
- When texting people for the first time, or those who don't have your name and number in their contacts listing or address books, be certain to introduce yourself and/or remind them of where you met. ("Hi, this is Scott, the business etiquette expert. For our chat at 11A about corporate training services, where would you like to connect?")
- Sexting – the practice of sending sexually explicit material, including nude photos or lascivious references – is unacceptable and inappropriate under any circumstance. A major high-tech breach of conduct, it may also lead to embarrassment or prosecution, and should be taken seriously by any employer.

**Borrowing a Device**
- Do not use someone's high-tech device without permission.
- If they have forgotten to do so, log them out of any social network, instant messenger, app or software program before you use it yourself.
- Getting permission to use a device does not give you the permission to snoop through other people's personal files, accounts, software or media.
- Under no circumstance is it acceptable to read open emails that others have created, or look through their inboxes or sent messages.
- Avoid visiting any risqué, controversial, or potentially harmful (i.e. spam or fraudulent) websites while on another's device.
- Ask permission before changing any device settings – even something as simple as WiFi connection point access – and restore everything back to the previous settings before returning the device.
- Do not change the lending party's home page, or delete or install new software, without their express permission. If you are finished using installed software, uninstall it before returning possession of the device to the lender.
- Try not to borrow someone's device if you're nursing a cold, flu or other potential health condition that could spread germs and sickness. If you must do so, observe appropriate health precautions (using hand sanitizer, turning away to cough, wiping down the device with a disinfecting cloth, etc.) before, during and after usage.

- Resist the temptation to access graphic content or inappropriate websites; your colleague might not use his iPad only to access email while on a business trip... he also might use it to entertain his three year-old son at a restaurant!
- Do not delete files or close open programs, windows and documents without others' permission. If you find closing a document to be unavoidable, be sure to save a version (e.g. "save as," not just "save," in the latter case potentially overwriting important data) before doing so.
- Some devices allow for multiple people to use separate user logins, such as Windows and Mac computers. Where such a feature exists, it's appropriate to log out of any other person's profile that is signed in and log back in with your own when using a shared device. That way, you have your own desktop, files and settings to work with.
- Clean up after yourself: If you have disturbed any items on someone's desk, or used up supplies, be sure to pick up after yourself and replace missing items before handing access back over.

### Sharing a Device

- Consider scheduling set times during which each user is allowed to use the device uninterrupted, and sticking to those times, to minimize conflict.
- Be respectful of others' needs, and prioritize usage based on sensibility. If someone must perform an important task (producing a presentation on deadline, faxing a key contract, filing an important work report, etc.) it should take precedence over less time-sensitive pursuits.
- Do not open or look through others' documents, files or multimedia without permission.
- Do not close others' open windows, programs, apps or documents without first checking with them.
- Do not save files to folders designated for others' private use.
- Do not delete others' files, programs or contacts without receiving their permission.
- If you must close a document or program, save a version (e.g. "save as," not just "save," in the latter case potentially overwriting important data) and/or save open tabs and files before doing so.
- Log other users out of any social network, app or software program before you use it yourself.
- Do not visit risqué, controversial, or potentially harmful websites, including high-risk URLs that may present heightened security threats.
- Make others aware before changing any device settings or making permanent adjustments that may affect their computing experience.
- Do not change the lending party's home page, or delete or install new software, without their express permission. If you are finished using installed software, uninstall it

before returning possession of the device to the lender.

- Healthiness and cleanliness are essential: The same rules contained under Borrowing a Device apply here.

### Breaking Negative High-Tech Habits

- If you must check your phone, tablet or mobile device regularly, decide on regular intervals at which this task will be performed (say, every half hour or hour) as opposed to obsessively checking the device every ten seconds.
- Be aware of certain activities that do not require your device to be turned on, or during which usage is discouraged, and enjoy being disconnected for that moment.
- Schedule at least one day a month where you do not turn on your devices or, at the very least, leave them off for the majority of the day.
- Avoid interrupting interactions with others to send texts, make calls or reference mobile devices.
- Turn away from the computer or cell phone when others address you, and maintain ongoing attention and eye contact during conversations.

## Business Travel and High-Tech Devices

### High-Tech Travel Tips

- Turn the volume down on Bluetooth earpieces or portable media and music players so as not to disturb others, and allow for situational awareness, so you can hear honking horns or others attempting to initiate conversation. Note that loud noises may

### 4 HIGH-TECH ETIQUETTE RULES TO LIVE BY

We asked Rich DeMuro (www.facebook.com/richontech), tech reporter for KTLA-TV Los Angeles and Tribune Television to share his list of essential technology dos and don'ts when using high-tech devices in public. Following are four rules that he highly recommends that today's technology users abide by:

1. Don't put your phone on the restaurant table if you are having a meal with someone important – and by important, I'm talking everyone from the guy you want to get a job from to your mom when she comes in town. Putting your phone on the table signals [the other party, saying] "I'm waiting for something more important to come along." Roughly 99.9% of all texts, calls and emails can wait an hour until you're done with your meal. If you really need to stay in touch, put your phone on vibrate in your pocket.

leak from headphones and earpieces if volume levels aren't sufficiently low.

• When viewing media in shared company or public spaces (i.e. on airplanes or subway cars), be aware of who's around you and may, accidentally or otherwise, be able to observe this content, especially if the information is marked as confidential.

• Maintain situational awareness when in motion. At no time should you be so transfixed by a screen that you cannot safely navigate. Staring at a screen while walking isn't just rude – it's also potentially dangerous to yourself and others, and can result in unexpected stumbles, collisions or even serious injury.

• Pay attention to screen brightness. Before turning on devices with light-up displays (i.e. smartphones and tablets) in darkened public environs such as dimly-lit airplane interiors, politely ask those situated nearby if doing so will disturb them. When utilizing these electronics, consider lowering default screen brightness levels to minimize potential disturbances, which also causes them to consume less power, extending battery life as well.

## During Meetings

### Using Devices During Meetings

• Turn devices off during meetings unless you are expecting a time-sensitive email or call.

• If you must take a call or receive a text during a meeting, be polite and let the organizer know in advance. Setting devices to vibrate will also prevent you from disturbing others.

• Should you need to take an important call, politely excuse yourself (if possible) and step out of the meeting room to conduct it, and keep volume levels low so as not to disturb those still present within.

2. If you do get a phone call in a place where you are in others' company, excuse yourself from the group before talking.

3. If you're in close quarters, don't talk as loudly as you would as if you were in your office with the door closed. As interesting as it might seem for others to hear a one-sided conversation, it's just kind of annoying.

4. Do us all a favor and keep your phone on vibrate in the most public places. As someone who is in the TV business and routinely in and out of studios all day, I keep my phone on silent/vibrate all day long, and I have yet to miss a huge call.

- Texting, sending emails and checking messages should happen only after meetings are finished, or during official breaks.
- At no time during meetings should devices be used for personal purposes, i.e. updating social networks.
- Consider keeping an alternative voice message on hand letting callers know that you're in a meeting and switching to it while you are occupied, so they don't feel that they've been left hanging.
- If you must use an app during a meeting, set your device to Airplane Mode so it won't accept any outside calls or disturbances, and turn sound effects and volume levels to off.

### Appropriate Ringer Settings
- Always turn your phone's ringer off when in a meeting.
- When a ringer is on vibrate, keep your phone in your hand or pocket to avoid disturbing others with table shakes.
- Depending on the model of cell phone that you own, your device may also offer the option to briefly flash to signal incoming calls instead of making potentially more disturbing vibrations or rings – a feature that may be worth using.

### When to Shut Devices Off
- If you have a phone specifically utilized for work purposes, turn it off and put it away at the end of the workday if possible.
- Do not bring your work phone to family occasions, dates and other intimate or shared group events without warning friends and family in advance, and/or sharing your reasoning, before it becomes a potential annoyance with the host and other guests, whom it may disturb.
- Turn your phone off if someone specifically requests that you do so, no questions asked.
- Be aware of any automated alarms you've set, as some devices may allow them to go off even when they are powered down, or set to vibrate.

## Devices and Employer's Rights

- Employers may have the right to track or listen to messages on work devices, so keep personal exchanges off of them.
- Employers reserve the right to reclaim any devices when you leave the organization, so back up all personal data (and only personal data) that is rightfully yours and transfer it elsewhere prior to surrendering possession.
- When using shared devices such as fax machines and copiers, it is appropriate to

only look at the cover sheet and name – not the actual contents of the transmission, which should be promptly handed over to the appropriate recipient.

- Experts recommend shutting off all devices a minimum of one hour prior to bedtime in order to improve chances of enjoying restful sleep.

## Online Shorthand Dictionary: A Glossary Of Common Terms

Abbreviated messages have been a part of our language since the Pony Express, but they've experienced a massive resurgence with the advent of high-tech communications tools like instant messenger programs, texting, and social networks. As with previous generations who sent telegrams, users of modern technology often try to compress as much information into as little space as possible. Some solutions, like Twitter, are actually specifically designed to facilitate the exchange of short messages, while others, like phone-to-phone texting, are limited in length by necessity because transmitting each character literally costs the carrier money.

The most popular messaging services today oftentimes happen to be some of the newest, like Twitter and GroupMe, but the lingo has changed very little from the earliest days of the Internet. Following is a guide to common high-tech slang, shorthand and abbreviations that should help you translate these missives back into common English.

### PHONE FOLLIES – HOW NOT TO USE YOUR CELL PHONE

Daniel Sieberg, author of The Digital Diet, shares one of the most awkward things you can do with your phone in public:

"In my book I call these types of gaffes "tech turds." One of the most damning is just dumping your smartphone on the table during a professional business meal. Perhaps when smartphones first became popular the act of doing so was almost a novelty. Now it's just plain rude. It's like you've invited a guest to the meal whose only role is to interrupt the conversation. If you MUST have your smart-phone out, then make reference to it and tell your colleagues that you'll only check it if the one urgent message or call comes in, otherwise you have their complete attention. Another game that works is getting everyone to put their smartphones in a pile in the center of the table. The first one who has to pick it up during the meal picks up the check."

- ABT: About
- Addy: Address
- BBL: Be back later
- BFF: Best friends forever
- BFN/B4N: Bye for now
- BRB: Be right back
- BKA: Better known as
- BTW: By the way
- CYA: See ya
- CYE: Check your email
- FB: Facebook
- FUBAR: F***** up beyond all recognition
- FML: F**** my life
- FTW: For the win! (something went extremely well)
- FYEO: For your eyes only
- G2G: Got to go
- GTFO: Get the f*** out
- GTK: Good to know
- IDK: I don't know
- IMHO: In my humble opinion
- IMO: In my opinion
- J/K: Just kidding
- K: OK
- Kewl: Cool
- L8R: Later (see you)
- LMAO: Laughing my a** off
- LMK: Let me know
- LOL: Laughing out loud
- noob: A newbie, or amateur
- OMG: Oh my gosh
- OTL: Out to lunch
- Pix: Pictures
- ROFL: Rolling on the floor laughing
- RT: (in) Real time
- RT (On Twitter): Retweet
- RTM: Read the manual
- SMH: Shake my head

- Srsly: Seriously?
- STFU: Shut the f*** up
- Thx: Thanks
- TL;DR: Too long; didn't read
- TTYL: Talk to you later
- WIIFM: What's in it for me?
- <3 : Love (a heart)
- :) : Smiley face
- :D : Big grin
- :( : Frown
- :P : Silly (tongue sticking out)
- :o : Surprise or shock

# VIDEOCONFERENCING

Videoconferencing can be used by businesses as a powerful communications tool to cut costs, reduce travel requirements and improve efficiency, even on a global scale. An especially helpful solution for distributed or virtualized workforces, videoconferencing allows working professionals to deliver presentations and enjoy real-time conferences over the Internet wherein meeting participants actually get to see each others' faces and expressions in real-time. Like teleconferencing (audio group chat) solutions, live video chats can be quite useful for planning meetings, connecting with clients, delivering new business pitches, giving sales presentations, engaging in other collaborative ventures and projects, and simply connecting on a much more personal level than a teleconference offers.  Online meetings and meeting solutions can likewise be used for purposes of project management, sales, marketing, training, team building, brainstorming and more. All can help you communicate more effectively, promote greater teamwork and get more immediate and tangible reactions to new projects and project developments.

To hold a videoconference, you need a computer (with a webcam and microphone, headset, or speaker) or mobile device which offers a built-in front facing video camera, microphone and speaker, as well as an active Internet connection. You'll also need a software program that provides video chat functionality, with several popular apps, programs and even social networks now able to support these capabilities, allowing meeting participants to participate in a virtual conference room where everyone can see each other on-screen. In addition to observing others who are being streamlined live online, viewers can often share what appears on their device's screen, slideshow presentations, videos, multimedia and more with other participants. In fact, some programs even allow multiple people to take notes, edit documents and simultaneously engage in collaborative work while conversing. Many meeting applications which support videoconferencing also offer teleconferencing or audio conferencing capability, which allows participants the option to participate by telephone or solely as an audio stream.

## Basic Rules

- Prepare as carefully for online meetings and treat them as you would in-person meetings – the informal veneer of video conferencing can be deceiving, but business exchanges must be handled with equal professionalism in both real and virtual life.
- Manners matter. Even the Emily Post Institute recommends remaining respectful of

dialogue, tone, posture, eye contact, cultural norms and other real-life concerns while virtually conversing.

- Dress appropriately for video chats and maintain corresponding standards of personal cleanliness and hygiene – your appearance should be professional, presentable and respectful.
- Refrain from foul language, abusive statements and negative commentary – comport yourself as you would in any polite, real-world face-to-face interaction.
- Test equipment before the big conference. Equipment malfunctions may still happen, but they will be minimized if you do some testing ahead of the big meeting.
- Should technical malfunctions occur, greet them with poise and aplomb – others are watching. Maintaining grace under pressure is important, as is having a backup plan.
- Clean up surrounding areas and backgrounds, as they will be visible on-camera. Be aware of any sensitive personal information that may unintentionally be revealed during recording by background objects that are visible in the frame, and make sure your surroundings are neat and professional.
- In select cases, it may be acceptable during videoconferences to drink water, juice or other caffeinated beverages suitable for consumption at office environments, but make sure doing so isn't a distraction. If it has the potential to become one, hold your thirst.
- Forget snacking, however: Food and cameras don't mix. Munching – especially while trying to talk and communicate – is distracting and can produce unattractive results (crumbs falling, mouths opening, loud lip smacking, etc.).
- Speak clearly and distinctly. Try not to mumble. Note that computer microphones and speakers may distort signals: It may be necessary to talk more loudly, and enunciate more than normal – however, it's best to ask the other party how signals are coming through before doing so.
- Lag, or signal delays, may also impact conversations – be sure to factor timing into exchanges so as not to talk over one another, miss important information or result in unintentional gaffes.
- Understand that while conversations may be casual, ramifications can be serious – watch what you say and do, as it's all too easy to record and share even what appear to be private conversations.
- Carry yourself as if all interactions were occurring in a public space – you never know who is watching.
- Set time limits and have an agenda to keep everyone on task and on track.
- When working collaboratively on projects, it's recommended that specific team members be assigned to specific tasks – e.g. recording notes, updating master project documents or jotting down action items – to minimize confusion and ensure that all team members are in sync.

- Though videoconferencing exchanges will occur virtually, note that all cultural norms and social mores expected from in-person exchanges should be taken into consideration and observed throughout them as well.

## The Importance of Training and Practice

- Prior to the actual event, practice your video conference and run new equipment through hands-on tests, so that employees know exactly what to expect and how things should work. A dress rehearsal can prevent opening night jitters and mistakes due to human error.
- While practice conferences will help prevent some technical snafus, some technical problems may still occur, due to the unpredictability of technology and data connections. Develop a contingency plan before they happen.
- During test sessions, you may be able to discern if participants aren't speaking clearly, loud enough or with enough enunciation to survive digital transmission – practices offer the opportunity to enhance their delivery of information.
- Bear in mind that default configuration settings may not suit your needs: Test conferences provide the perfect opportunity to adjust microphone levels, camera positioning and transmission capabilities so as to avoid any issues the day of the actual event.

## Getting Your Office Onboard With Videoconferencing

- Sometimes changing from a schedule of travel-intensive real-world meetings to virtual communications and videoconferencing tools can be challenging for certain employees: Concerns should be addressed, and extensive hands-on education and training provided, prior to day-of events.
- Businesses are advised to adopt videoconference-specific policies so that employees know what to expect from sessions, and appropriate rules for conducting and comporting themselves.
- Schedule regular educational briefings, hands-on development sessions and software updates across your network to ensure systems, software programs and skill sets are in sync – employees should be up to speed on videoconferencing solutions, and all should be standardized throughout your offices.
- When conducting virtual gatherings, keep your surroundings as similar to that of those you'd encounter during real-world meetings. According to certain studies, businesspeople are more comfortable using videoconferencing solutions when the environment presented is similar to that of an in-person meeting.

## When to Videoconference or Teleconference

- When an in-person meeting isn't possible and – in the case of videoconferencing –

when a phone call doesn't suffice, or more personal face-to-face interaction is required.

- When you need to see each other, e.g. to gauge others' reactions or establish rapport, and when it's imperative that the subtle nuances and personality that live conversation conveys be employed, so as not to lose them in electronic translation.
- When it pays to show or share: Videoconferences are tremendously useful when engaging in highly visual forms of communication, and when it helps to see and/or share what others are seeing, i.e. to minimize confusion or demonstrate product or service functionality.
- When you need to collaborate, build a more personal connection with others, or visually present documents or media, but distance presents a barrier.
- When you need to bring together people and partners in geographically disparate locations.
- When you want to conduct live demonstrations.

**When NOT to Video Conference**
- When the subject being discussed is sensitive or confidential in nature.
- When emotion, office politics or finer points best conveyed in person are involved – face-to-face is more respectful and genteel.
- When visual elements of the discussion are less important, or it's best to give others time to digest and process information before they respond – in these cases, an email, phone call or text may suffice.
- When all participants are situated closely enough together to allow for actual face to face interactions, and time permits: Videoconferencing shouldn't be looked to as a substitute for otherwise easily accomplished interpersonal exchanges.
- When there is the need to discuss formal matters or topics of extreme gravity (e.g. in the event of downsizings) and only informal settings are available.

# EMAIL

Email remains one of the most popular high-tech ways of doing business or communicating with colleagues and clients, and among the most widely utilized solutions that's also accessible from a variety of electronic devices. You may be happy to note that given the medium's widespread public familiarity, despite the rise in popularity of texting and social networking, it still enjoys a commanding presence in the marketplace: In fact, an estimated 300 billion emails are sent every day! Regardless of the huge volume of messages exchanged on an ongoing basis though, many missives suffer from basic issues such as the sharing of inappropriate content, conversational miscommunications, and users' willingness to buy into common communications myths. Still the premier way of communicating for many users, however, proper email etiquette remains as vital as ever.

## General Tips

• Email is a common source of miscommunication, because tone, context and subtle nuances are easily lost in translation. Before sending, consider if your commentary could be misconstrued and/or misinterpreted, and if a simple phone call might be better advised.

• Likewise, truly important or time-sensitive queries may be best addressed via a call, given email's periodic propensity to be delayed or misrouted by touchy servers and spam filters.

• Once written, emails cannot be undone – watch what you say, whom you copy, and always think twice before sending them along.

• Don't write anything in an email that you wouldn't be comfortable saying in person – or in public. Easily forwarded and shared, and/or monitored by employers, inappropriate commentary may come back to haunt you. Professionalism is imperative.

• Unless you get a response, don't assume that emails have been received – Internet issues, inbox filters and even simple misspellings of email addresses may result in communications going awry.

• Be careful (and be careful to double-check recipients) when copying and blind carbon copying: A slip of the keyboard, finger or auto-completing contact form may inadvertently send messages to the wrong party, or result in dozens of parties' contact information accidentally being shared with one another.

• When sending to multiple recipients, consider blind carbon copying for courtesy's sake, or creating groups of users, which shield recipients contained in the group from seeing who else has been copied.

- If you're going to add people to the email conversation, let recipients know ("I'm copying John Smith, our head of marketing, here.")
- For courtesy's sake, subject lines should be short, sweet and directly relate to email contents: Misleading or false statements, or needlessly open-ended or misleading questions ("Did you hear about...?") will be poorly received.
- Before marking emails as urgent, tantamount to putting an underscore under your message in someone's inbox, genuinely ask yourself: Will the other party consider the query just as important as I do? If not, they may rush to read something that didn't need urgent prioritizing, and be understandably irritated.
- Before hitting "Reply All" – which sends messages to all individuals copied on an email, not just the sender – consider whether it's important for everyone to receive your response.
- Remember that some things are best left unsaid, and you don't always have to have the last word: Cut down on spam by avoiding pointless responses or sly replies that keep conversations going when they've naturally ended.
- Courtesy suggests that we be timely about responding to emails – most responses should happen within 24 hours. Should you lack time to respond that soon, it's recommended that you at least send a brief note letting senders know when a proper response will be forthcoming. ("So sorry, I've been tied up with a last-minute deadline – I'll drop you a line by the end of this week.")
- When away from your desk for travel or vacations, set an out of office response stating when you'll return, and the conditions under which you may or may not be checking your inbox. ("Thanks for your email. I'm out of office on business until Friday, March 2nd, but will be checking messages periodically. Please be advised that some correspondence may be delayed, but I'll get back to you as soon as possible.")
- Free email services are plentiful, but be aware that some may display ads based on keywords found within your correspondence, or may be perceived as being less acceptable or professional than dedicated website email addresses. Use of services such as Gmail is becoming more common, however, and surrounding attitudes are rapidly changing.
- When receiving a suspicious email from a service or provider you use, visit the actual company website and log in to research the issue as opposed to rather than directly clicking on any links contained within the email. Similarly, never dial the numbers contained within suspicious messages, but rather call those directly retrieved from the company's official website.
- If you feel compelled to share sensitive info (never a wise choice), use utmost discretion or, ideally, let others know prior to sharing direct quotes or private conversations with a third party.
- Never give out your email account information, login or password to another party. If

you do, request that they inform you as soon as they are finished using it, and then promptly change your password.

- Resist the impulse to use emoticons (characters such as smiley faces used to denote tone or mood), except for the most casual and informal of interactions.
- Ditch the dirty jokes, photos and videos.

## Basics

### Addressing Subjects

- Dear XXX is largely outdated, and too intimate for casual email communications – a simple "Hello Joe" or "Hi Jane," will suffice in most instances.
- When addressing unknown parties, "To Whom It May Concern" is standard.
- Try to attain a professional tone. Overly flowery or formal emails may be as off-putting as uncomfortably casual missives are.

### How to Close Emails

- "Sincerely" and "Yours truly" may be commonplace within hand-written letters, but best saved for only serious email communications. You might consider using "Regards" or "Best" as closers instead.
- Automatic signatures are OK, but shouldn't be overly intrusive – a name, job title/business name, address, email address and phone number should provide enough room to get your point across. Anything more is overkill – inspirational quotes and rainbow colors included.
- Within reason, it's best to avoid referencing religious, political and negatively-inclined quotes (or those that may be perceived as critical or judgmental) in email signatures, as they may lessen the appearance of professionalism in the eyes of certain viewers.

### The Best Time to Email

- It is rude to email someone with an invitation for a professional event the same day it occurs unless circumstances truly prohibit earlier contact, and/or there is an established understanding between you and the person.
- Sending late-night emails may be necessary at times, but do be aware that recipient's devices may make noises when one is received, potentially disturbing them.
- Note that emails received at odd times – weekends, early AM hours, etc. – may send the proverbial wrong message to the recipient. Ex: Why was he or she working at 3AM – let alone thinking I'd be on the job then? Be cognizant of differences between time zones and territories.

## What is Appropriate and Inappropriate to Email

• Attachments are OK to include, but emails should always include a description or heads-up of what's being attached. Note that sending attachments the first time you correspond with someone may be seen as suspicious. Also, it's possible that emails containing attachments or links will be seen as spam, so if possible, alert the recipient that you are sending such an email, either by phone, text or a "clean" email, and that they might want to check their spam/junk folder as well.

• Never click on unexpected or unsolicited attachments, which may contain viruses, Trojans, malware or other harmful contents.

• Do not send inappropriate jokes, photos or attachments that are inappropriate.

• Do not send personal emails from a professional address.

• Do not give your business email to friends and relatives who will use it inappropriately.

• Do not send sensitive information or documents to people or businesses that your manager would not approve of.

• Do not forward proprietary work messages without getting approval first.

## Tone of Voice

• Writing in capital letters is the virtual equivalent of yelling: SO CONSIDER CUTTING IT OUT, M'KAY?

• Sarcasm, wry humor, and other nuanced styles can easily be misinterpreted over email – cut to the chase, and be straightforward in email communications.

• Grammatical errors, problems with punctuation and spelling issues will reflect poorly in viewers' eyes – always give messages a second pass before hitting Send.

• Along similar lines, be cognizant of the attitude you're portraying and appropriateness of the content being discussed – if you wouldn't feel comfortable stating the contents of the message aloud in a public workplace setting, don't say them in an email either.

## Avoiding Miscommunications

• It is OK to follow up crucially important or deadline-oriented emails with a phone call or a text.

• Emoticons shouldn't be used often, but they can help convey your meaning if you fear being misunderstood.

• Some email clients allow the use of italics, bold characters or underscoring to emphasize turns of phrase. If unavailable, putting asterisks around important notes (as a reminder, *don't forget to pick me up at *9AM Eastern at Terminal 4, please*) may substitute to designate emphasis or importance in their place.

• Return receipts – notifications that confirm when an email is received and read –

may appear overly aggressive, or give recipients the impression that you feel they're untrustworthy. Avoid using wherever possible, except when messages are of the utmost urgency.

### Using 'Reply to All' Features
- Think before copying everyone on an email and ask yourself before sending: Do they really need to receive this message? If no company exists, it's best to avoid sending. Doing so can help you minimize distraction and clutter for others.
- Be careful when copying others on email, especially with regard to sensitive data – auto-complete features of email programs make it all too easy to inadvertently copy the wrong parties.
- As conversations progress, cease copying those for whom they are no longer relevant as both of sign of courtesy and consideration.

## Professional Guidelines

### The Best Time to Email/Using Scheduled Emails
- Business emails should, wherever possible, be confined to working hours – unless you're working in different time zones and/or continents, recipients may be understandably perplexed to receive emails from you at 2AM.
- Monday morning and Friday afternoon are often the worst times to reach out since people are slammed at the beginning of the week and rushing to meet the closing buzzer before the weekend.
- Tuesday and Thursday may be the most productive work days and may yield the best results in terms of response rates.
- Some busy people clear out their email inboxes on Sunday night when they're free from disturbances before the work week begins. However, it is often inappropriate to contact them over the weekend – while you may not expect them to read messages until Monday morning, recipients may be offended when their leisure time is interrupted by what's perceived to be an urgent work request.
- If you are ceasing employment with an organization, it is OK send an email update giving your contacts a heads-up and providing new personal contact information, which should always be professional and neutral or upbeat in tone. (You should also setup an automatic response making senders aware that you are no longer at the job, and whom to reach out to in your absence.) However, it is not appropriate to discuss new employers or provide contact information for your new position through a previous employer's email network.

### Knowing When to CC, BCC, etc.

• Shift people to carbon copy (CC) when you don't want them to have to receive every email exchange, but want them to be aware that the conversation is happening.

• Be careful blind carbon copying (BCCing) people, as they could copy, paste, and reply to recipients that weren't aware that a third-party saw the email in the first place.

• Don't include others on email chains unless there's an important reason for them to be involved in the conversation — otherwise, you'll just clutter up their inbox.

### Establishing a Respectable Signature

• Automatic signatures should be short and sweet: Keep them limited to a name, job title, business name, address, email address, phone number and possibly company logo. Anything more, or more heavy-handed, may be seen as unprofessional.

• Your signature should link to your professional website(s), not to your social network or personal sites.

• The shorter your signature, the better.

• Once you get a response to an email, remember to delete your signature before your next response to keep the same information from needlessly repeating multiple times.

### Not Being a Spammer

• Don't automatically add users to mass email lists without requesting their advance permission.

• All mass communications should include an unsubscribe option that's just one click away — and not request added steps like retyping one's email address, clicking menu options, or explaining why they've opted out of your communications.

• Always be honest in the purpose of your email, including providing references to information contained within if needed, and being transparent about where outside links will send the reader.

• Avoid sending unsolicited attachments since they consume recipients' email storage space, may be viewed as suspicious, and highly increase the chance your email will be caught in their spam filter.

• When sending mass emails, use solutions that refer to recipients by first name — but be certain names appear in the same color, font and size as the rest of the message, so the fact that it's a faceless form letter isn't obvious.

### Following Up on Emails

• It is fine to follow up on deadline-oriented emails shortly after sending, though it is usually best to do so via another form of communication like a phone call or text message.

## BEING RESPONSIBLE WITH ONLINE SEARCHES

It's a unique time: We can learn nearly everything there is to know about everyone nowadays – at least, the details that are worth mentioning online – just by using a search engine. Google, Bing, Ask.com and other Internet services have revolutionized how we research. But the question they present is how to utilize this information while still respecting others' boundaries. A few tips that may help you conduct ethical online searches follow:

• Many view it as fair game to research a potential employer, client, or trade partner online when considering working together, or starting a new strategic relationship. But consider how much digging is appropriate – do you really need to see family photos, or know every last intimate detail about what they do in their off-hours? Let logic be your guide.

• Tread carefully when bringing up controversial information found in a Google search with other parties, as data may be false, misleading, unrepresentative of actual character and professional

• Be as aware as possible of the recipient's actual access to email (e.g. whether they're on vacation or in a meeting), and be respectful of their time: They may be too busy to get back to you immediately.

• There's no hard and fast rule on when to follow up on emails, but for personal interactions, once every three days may be appropriate – and once every four to five days for business interactions. Alternating communications types (i.e. following up an email with a phone call) between contact attempts may prove helpful.

### Tone of Voice

• Terse emails can unintentionally come off as angry, just as sending long-winded or rambling emails can seem disrespectful of a person's time.

• Keep humor and double entendres to a minimum, especially when addressing someone you haven't worked with before, as they may be viewed as unprofessional.

• If you know the person in real life, consider their individual forms of tone and speech as you're reading their emails – it may help you interpret messages, and better understand the sender's mindset.

• When composing important or high-stakes emails, write them out, save them as drafts, and then read them aloud later and apply revisions before you hit Send. It's always smart to give crucial messages a second read-through.

### Appropriate Emails

• Personal commentary and discussions should take place outside of work hours and work-related inboxes.

• Get a personal email address and utilize it in lieu of using your work email address to handle party invitations, social network interactions, contact with friends and other personal needs.

- When responding to mass emails, unless there's a pressing need to converse with all copied parties, do not use the Reply All option instead of replying directly to the party who sent the message.

**Adding Users to Mailing Lists**
- Explicitly ask permission before adding someone to your email blasts.
- Keep your frequency of email blasts reasonable – although the definition of "reasonable" differs, a maximum of one outreach attempt a week, or every two weeks, makes a good starting point. Note that sending multiple emails of this nature or repeats of past outreach efforts may annoy and aggravate recipients.
- Make it easy to unsubscribe from email blasts, whether it be via a simple reply email or a one-touch online button or contact form – no more than a single action step should be required.

values, or relate to issues that the person may not feel comfortable speaking about, or would prefer to discuss at another time.
- Google yourself and see what online history you can discover, and consider whether you feel it's ethical trying to scrub any dirt away before others find it. However, it is wholly appropriate to ask that offensive, false, misleading or needlessly defamatory posts be removed, and to take steps to lower their search result rankings. Note that Google has historically made a point of not actively stepping in and modifying search results.
- Create a Google Alert based on a series of keywords (i.e. your name or business' name), and Google will contact you whenever your name, your organization's name, or another related topic comes up on the web, allowing you to stay on top of related postings.
- Consider that there are likely multiple people and businesses who share the same or similar names before confronting a person with something you found online that you believe is related to you or your organization.

# BLOGS, WEBSITES AND ONLINE NEWSGROUPS

Over the past decade, websites have rapidly begun to supplant office water coolers, newspapers and magazines as the place to share the latest news, opinions and gossip. The speed of today's news cycle and at the rate at which stories proliferate online is part of the equation, but websites also give readers the opportunity to respond quickly, anonymously and in often highly-opinionated fashion. The downside being, of course, that we don't always have the time to fully think through our responses as we did in the days of snail mail and handwritten letters.  This can be especially problematic for businesses – either by way of when employees communicate in ways that are unprofessional or when anonymous customers badmouth a corporation or product. Businesses sometimes even find themselves tussling with others online who may or may not share their viewpoints, who enjoy the pleasure of harassing others, or who simply do not have the company's best interests at heart. Knowing this, and recognizing that these resources are shared public spaces, observing certain rules of conduct and manners when utilizing blogs, websites and online newsgroups is therefore vital for businesses and their employees.

## General Tips

### Rules of Conduct

• Some websites, newsgroups and blogs touch on popular themes and memes; others are purely personal or promotional spaces. Rules of behavior and engagement vary – it's imperative to reference and respect each site's posting and contribution guidelines before joining the conversation.

• Just as you wouldn't jump into a dialogue with strangers without first observing the discussion to gain a sense of propriety and context, don't dive right into online forums, especially if you are doing so to promote yourself or your company. Before contributing, sit back and study how others act (including actual posts, tone of voice, the way in which users interact, and the reactions these interactions prompt) to understand appropriate social norms and the site's overall rules of behavior.

• Promotional posts and advertisements are inappropriate to post at any time outside of appropriately-designated channels. That said, if it fits within the site's social context, a short mention of something you've worked on or contributed may be appropriate in passing conversation ("Thanks, Sarah – here are some handy resources for keeping kids safe online. If you're interested in high-tech etiquette, you might also want to check out this new guide we've written.") However, it's best to do so in the context of requesting others' feedback, thoughts or opinions – not trying to close a sale.

- Spamming other users is not acceptable under any circumstance.

## How to Join a Blog Conversation
- Be polite and respectful of others' thoughts and opinions.
- Do not make rude, false or inappropriate statements, including those specifically intended to incite other users.
- Commentary, ideas and points that you're looking to make should be clearly written and spelled out, and facts concisely presented and appropriately referenced or linked to as needed.
- Proper spelling and grammar should be used when entering posts.
- Read what people have posted carefully before commenting. There are few worse things than misinterpreting or missing something that someone said, or repeating comments already made by another user.
- It's always smart to refer to the original post, or quote from prior commentary being referenced, to make it clear that you have read and comprehended the piece and subsequent discussion points.
- Ask yourself: What can I contribute to the conversation? Then do so. If you can't add relevant information, statements or viewpoints of value, perhaps it's better left unsaid?
- Relevancy matters – stay on-topic for the site and thread, and consider whether the information being shared is something other individuals would actually be interested in reading.

## Being a Responsible Contributor
- Name calling, cursing or being argumentative not only creates ill will, but often makes others discount your opinion.
- Logging in or providing an actual name (not posting anonymously) is encouraged, as attribution implies that you stand behind your statements, and are willing to be held accountable for what you say.
- Stay within the realm of the blog's chosen topic of focus, even if other contributors stray from the subject at-hand.
- Treat other contributors with respect, dignity and consideration, just as you would if you were having a conversation with them at a cocktail party or social event.

## Tone of Voice, Rules of Conduct and Posting Frequency
- Posting multiple replies before others can contribute looks odd and amateurish – after posting, give others time to respond before leaving additional comments.
- Follow the style and parameters of the blog and its posters, recognizing that a snarky pop culture website may observe different rules of tone, voice and conduct than a serious medical journal.

- Rather than fire off responses immediately, it's often best to wait to reply to a comment challenging your opinion, in order to offer a more well thought out and appropriate response.
- Most major blogs have a rules of conduct or terms of service page – familiarize yourself with house rules before you begin posting.

## Avoiding Self-Promotion

- As a rule, self-aggrandizing or self-promotional posts should generally be avoided. If you intend to do so, any comments made to this effect should be made as "we" vs. "I," and must be directly related to the post or discussion thread and in some way provide value to your fellow readers. ("Check out this cool website we just finished, which offers a lot of hints and tips that may help answer your questions about netiquette (sorry, shameless self promotion, we know... ).")
- Assume that if people wanted to hear your life story or your company's complete history, you would be running the blog, not commenting on it.
- If you create a profile for blog postings, add a one-sentence signature (at most) with a link to your website or brand. Avoid using a giant logo or shot of your product or brand as a profile photo or companion image.
- Avoid attaching pictures or other bandwidth-hogging multimedia to your blog replies, and do not randomly insert plugs for or links to your products or projects.

## How to Be Critical and Insightful, But Not Confrontational

- If you are discussing facts, stick to the facts. Do not post misleading or untrue statements.
- If you are discussing experiences, make it clear that it is your personal experience, not necessarily a universal experience.
- If you are accused of making things up, politely and respectfully provide references and links to relevant topics or supporting data.
- Be to the point, avoiding personal jabs or attacks.
- Always consider how others may interpret your commentary and actions before posting, and whether it's best to clarify points up-front to avoid possible miscommunication.
- Keep it clean. It's fine to disagree with someone, but do so in a respectful way that clearly outlines your own viewpoint.
- Avoid name-calling, argumentativeness and labeling.

## Dealing With Argumentative Bullies, Known as "Trolls"

- Trolls assume that you want to win every Internet argument and that you aren't going to walk away from one, even as they post statements intended to provoke and incite. Ignoring them is often the best approach: It's hard to keep the flames stoked if you don't help feed the fire.

- Make site moderators and owners aware of the troll's negative actions, which may be in violation of site policy.
- Consider backing away from the troll and not responding. By doing so, you may potentially defuse conflicts by refusing to provide fuel for the quarrel, which can often lead harassers to tire of arguing with themselves. Likewise, as a result of their ineffectual squabbles, trolls may accidentally reveal their true intentions, be silenced by other commentators tired of their behavior, or even wind up banned or blocked from the site by its moderators.
- Be aware of your own behavior, as you may be tempted to tease or bait an emotional commentator on a blog.

## Conduct Within Forums

- Contribute to conversations that are helpful to other people, but aren't always self-serving or related to personal interests.
- Read as many posts on the forum as possible to better understand the culture of the venue before posting or responding yourself.
- Remember that everything posted online is permanent, and will reflect upon you.
- Always be honest and up-front, even if you think no one will find out that you made something up.
- Log in and create a profile on the forum, as this makes you more trustworthy than an anonymous poster.

## Maintaining a Professional Image

- Fill out your online profile and details before you begin posting, and be sure it's in keeping with the same image you present on the job – including using a professional photo of yourself as an associated image.
- Keep all postings and profiles respectful and professional – their appearance will be seen as representative of your personal demeanor, character and conduct.
- Understand that you are representing your company at all times in any public space, even if you are sharing a personal opinion.
- Treat everyone with respect and dignity, as you would in any professional situation.

## Contacting People Through Unusual Channels

- Directly reaching out to individuals for personal or work-related matters through a public forum such as blog post or newsgroup response is awkward at best. Whenever possible, look for a public or work-related website of theirs that freely volunteers a contact form or work email address, and use these channels for outreach.

- Do not try to reach potential employers for direct job-related queries through their personal blogs. In certain specific cases, it is, however, acceptable to contact them to discuss posts of theirs you've read, topics they've expressed interest in or other public statements that they've made, provided the context strictly relates to the publicly-viewable item in question. Note that this may lead into a more natural dialogue during which your interest in potential employment may come up. However, such discussion must occur organically – direct outreach via personal spaces regarding immediate purposes of employment or lead generation is a breach of etiquette.
- Access journalists and other professionals only through the channels that they personally designate and assume that if they want to contact you, they will contact you back.

## ONLINE AND SOCIAL CORPORATE ETIQUETTE

Gary Davis, vice president of global consumer marketing at McAfee, says that corporations and businesses can win or lose big with customers, depending on their capacity for proper online etiquette. Here's his advice for connecting and conversing with customers in a more professional manner:

**Q:** What basic rules for corporate online etiquette should businesses be observing?

**A:** First, you need to make sure that you engage your audience in a dialogue. This isn't about pushing information out and hoping people will consume it: It's about having a discussion, right? Information needs to be setup in a way that allows for feedback and discussion.

Second, you need to be authentic. As much we love to think we can just spew "marketing speak" at things, your dialogue needs to be as transparent as possible. I think that's very important to remember, because throwing up false pretenses does more damage than good.

Third, you need to be timely. The last thing you can afford is to engage [customers] in dialogue then act like it doesn't matter. I remember a couple of years ago when I went to a wireless carrier's forums and asked a question about a piece of software. They got back to me nine months later. At that point, they were better off just not answering at all because they looked like stooges for answering so late.

Everything we do today happens at the speed of the Internet. It's all about consistency, regularity, and the cadence of having that dialogue.

**Q:** How can a company best promote itself online through social media — and who in the organization should be the one responding to questions and engaging with the public? Also, how often should you be communicating?

**A:** I think you do it as often as is relevant and meaningful. What you don't want to do is just spam stuff out there ad nauseum because then you're going to lose relevancy. Posts need to be timely, and be done at a cadence that's not going to overwhelm, because people just can't consume that much information. As far as interaction goes, that depends on discussion. There are some matters that really require the response of a subject matter expert or a leader, and there are other things that can be answered by almost anyone—it depends on the competence or skills of your people.

**Q:** When you are trying to have a conversation with customers, how do you make sure you're responding respectfully if you're barraged with opinions and insights? Case in point: Who and what do you respond to if five thousand people are talking and some of them take umbrage?

**A:** Some people are very vocal—they'll respond over and over again, and be very active. In these cases, being temperate in your response is probably the right approach. There's no way you can respond to everybody. You need to ask yourself, what are the main themes or thoughts that are coming through? Look for those, and respond to those. You certainly don't want to get confrontational and open up dialogue for debate on a forum that may not be best for a debate. Social media, at least the way we use it, isn't a great platform for debate—it's more for education and sharing information that consumers will benefit from.

**Q:** What are the best, most efficient, and most powerful ways to promote your business online?

**A:** The two things I always turn to are media relations and social interaction. We recently did our Most Dangerous Celebrities Campaign. We had 500 broadcast tips, and thousands of tweets about it coming from a lot of the celebrities that were mentioned as part of the study. That's the sort of thing that I think consumers really benefit from. For example, when Jimmy Kimmel spends five minutes of his show talking about this study, it really resonates. We did the study, and since he was the top male celebrity, he gets some mileage of his own. To me, that's the best thing we can do.

Second to that is social media. I generally believe that people tend to buy depending on what their friends on social media are doing and saying. Historically, we've worked closely with industry pundits at outlets like PC Magazine and CNET, because that's where people would go to decide where they should buy their next anti-virus product, for example. We're finding more and more people are looking to their social network for recommendations. If all my friends are buying Hondas, maybe I'll go buy a Honda as my next car, right? I think we're going to see a higher degree of buying behaviors being influenced by social networks.

**Q:** What role do you think that many businesses and brands should play on social media and outreach channels? Creator, curator of news, pollster... perhaps even all of the above?

**A:** It's really all of the above. Infographics are a big part of this: Consumers really love to see meaningful information presented in a way that they can easily relate to. Polling and doing surveys and doing other types of activities are good, too. If all you do is insert yourself in the conversation or try and start a discussion, that's going to come across as too limiting in scope and you're not going to be afforded the opportunity that having more diverse and integrated campaigns can bring.

# CORPORATE BLOGGING AND SOCIAL MEDIA OUTREACH

## Corporate Blogging

Most major companies from AT&T to Zippo now boast corporate blogs, which serve as vital source of communication with customers, whether those customers are end users or other businesses. But before you jump on the bandwagon, you might want to consider a few pointers with regard to high-tech etiquette. All can save potential headaches and hassle, and help ensure exchanges with other parties are more positive.

### Start with a Plan, and Make a Lasting Commitment to Your Audience

• Don't assume that effective online communication is a task that can be delegated to just anyone in your organization. Maintaining proper respect for readers necessitates the use of strong communications skills – outreach directly impacts brand perception, and being representative of such, should be treated with utmost care and respect. While contributors can come from every facet of the organization, all posts they contribute should create value for customers, be well-written and grammatically sound, and convey both a professional tone and image.

• Keep your corporate goals at the forefront of all communications, and post items in keeping with both these objectives and brand image. Posts shouldn't be overtly self-promotional, but should speak to the stated mission of the business and blog, and – most importantly – be relevant to the reader. Consider your objective: Is it to increase sales, build a brand, or connect with customers? Whatever goal you decide upon will drive your content strategy – while posts may differ in nature and format, all should be in keeping with these designs.

• Remember that all blogs, bloggers and brands have a professional personality – only post items in keeping with them, and craft tone and dialogue to match. Although a powerful way to humanize an organization and build empathy, unless it's a recognized facet of its public persona, or the organization is specifically looking to shift perceptions, you'll want to be judicious with the use of humor, for example.

• Launching any public communications platform – especially blogs, which are meant to be read on a recurring and regular basis – is a commitment. Expect creating and maintaining one to take significant time and resources, and allocate manpower and budget accordingly – a steady supply of recurring content is necessary to keep viewers returning. Note that a daily posting schedule may require that at least one employee spend anywhere from 30 to 90 minutes on average researching, writing and posting the blog. Establishing a posting frequency is important, as is keeping up with it:

Randomly step away from the conversation for weeks at a time, and you may find it difficult to draw readers back.

• Don't be discouraged if your blog posts don't immediately garner thousands of page views upon launch. It takes time to build an audience, but focusing on quality content is the best way to begin doing that.

### Make Sure You Serve Customers' Interests, Not Just Your Own

• Keep self-promotion to a minimum: While announcements, press releases and other corporate news can be of interest to readers, the focus of a corporate blog should not strictly be on advertising – rather, sharing information of use to end-users.

• Wherever possible, look for ways to balance promotional postings with content of other kinds: While there's no hard and fast gauge here, as a general rule, at least 80% of postings should be focused away from pure marketing plays.

• Look for ways to create value for readers – e.g. by providing inside or exclusive information, sharing access to special deals and opportunities, or simply making readers aware of new trends, developments and insights related to your industry.

• The best corporate blogs don't simply rehash news or information: They create it, or add unique perspectives to the conversation. Figure out what topics your customers are most interested in – then provide postings which speak to them in a language that all can appreciate and understand.

• Note that customers should have a voice in the conversation: Dialogue shouldn't simply work one way, and feedback and comments must be acknowledged.

### Communicating with Personality Doesn't Mean Being Unprofessional

• Just because your blog is written in an easy-to-understand, lively, human voice doesn't mean it should be glib, trite or condescending. Watch what you say as well: All should be appropriate for conversation in a professional context – if you wouldn't say it around the office, don't say it publicly on the Internet either. Treat audiences with dignity, respect and professionalism – how you comport yourself reflects directly on your brand.

• Stay on topic, and make your posts about subjects of interest to readers – not about yourself. Corporate channels should never be seen as a platform for individuals to be self-aggrandizing. Always remember that they exist to serve customers – not one's ego.

• How you present yourself here is vital, as it reflects on your company's image: Spelling, grammatical and technical errors may lessen brand perception in the eyes of certain viewers.

• Beware of language, viewpoints and tone in posts that are inconsistent with your company's values and image. All contributors serve as brand ambassadors, and all contributions will be seen as tacitly endorsed by your organization when shared through official channels. Be cognizant of the impression and image that each is presenting.

- Always strive for clarity and ease of consumption: Communicating clearly and succinctly is crucial to connecting with your audience. Blogs that are too technical, for example, may confuse customers or lead to reader attrition. Consider your audience whenever creating posts, and tailor commentary to them.

### Blog From Your Company's Strengths

- Be unique and insightful – to maximize chances of success, stick to the topics your organization and subject matter experts know best, and present insights and commentary in a singular manner. The goal should be to always provide content readers can't get elsewhere.
- Fresh perspectives are vital: To make meaningful contributions to online conversations, it's important to add information, insights or a unique viewpoint. Simply parroting what others are doing brings little new to the discussion, and therefore provides little incentive for customers to comment upon or share such postings.
- Make sure your blog and all postings align with and relate to your brand and content strategy goals, helping to further enhance or establish your image. Not all should be overtly promotional – however, each should serve your stated professional purpose.
- Don't worry about keeping up with the Joneses. You don't need to run pricey contests, fancy giveaways or celebrity endorsements to get ahead online: Instead, think of ways you can create singular value for readers that they can't obtain from other sources.

### Create All Content for Sharing

- All content – blog posts, white papers, infographics, video commentary, interviews – and postings should be designed for online sharing to maximize outreach efforts. The ability to share content via social media heightens value and interest for customers (and provides possible incentive for pass-along), as well as affords search engine ranking improvements and one-click access to content via incoming links.
- Where possible, invite users to participate by sharing ideas, insights and content, and publicly acknowledge and thank them for participation – your community is your most powerful online contributor, and should be afforded equal standing and respect.
- Requesting posts from guest or community experts can be a powerful way to enhance brand image, content catalogue and relationships with third-parties: Don't be afraid to reach out. However, it's important to both be respectful of others (e.g. preserving the integrity and substance of their posts throughout any edits, providing photos/bios/linkbacks, and helping them cross-promote the appearance) and ask that

they be equally respectful of your business' guidelines in any such exchange.

- To ease navigation and improve traffic, always link to your main page, supporting sharing tools, and pertinent social media accounts – contact information, additional content and sharing options should always be one-click away.
- Note that many readers may land on individual blog posts, having discovered your site via search engines, rather than arriving on your main page – wherever possible, incoming visitors should be provided easy access to your blog or corporate website's homepage, and additional content of interest.

## CORPORATE BLOGGING DOs AND DON'Ts

Setting up a corporate blog can be a challenge, even for the most social media-savvy businesses – but it's one that your organization can certainly overcome, much to both its' and end-users' benefit. Melissa Zieger, influencer relations director for HP, points out several of the challenges, provides advice for making the most of your online channels and shares best practices for corporate blogging below.

**Q:** The best and worst ways companies often use official blogs and communities include?

**A:** A company blog can be a very effective way to enjoy a direct dialogue with your customers, but it needs to be a dialogue – not a monologue. At HP, we listen to reader feedback and review the metrics to see what content is resonating with our readers, and we take these into consideration when building new content. There are many things you can do to create a successful blog, but fundamentally, it is key to under-stand the audience that the blog/community is reaching and create content that is meaningful to them.

**Q:** What are the rules corporate bloggers should abide by?

Start with a topic you are knowledgeable and passionate about – successful blogs take time to develop, and it will be easier to sustain momentum if you write about a topic you really care about. My advice:
1)   Keep it simple and use proper grammar – Use language that novice readers, as well as experts, can understand.
2)   Develop an authentic "voice" – Be yourself, and develop your own point of view.
3)   Blog regularly – At least twice a week as a bare minimum.
4)   Admit (and fix) mistakes – Most people are not expecting perfection, just honesty.

**Q:** What are the most frequent mistakes that corporate bloggers make?

**A:** One of the most common mistakes is that people underestimate how much time blogging takes. People love the idea of contributing to a blog, but good writing takes time and dedication. And no one wants to see a corporate blog that hasn't been updated in months.

**Q:** What tone of voice, personality and approach should you use when posting publicly to corporate blog or website channels?

**A:** It depends upon the blog. The HP small business (SMB) blog has a different tone and personality than our consumer blog, for example. Determine what the tone and personality of your blog is and then find the right contributors that are a good fit.

**Q:** How do you create compelling content for corporate websites, blogs and other channels, and balance the need to engage and entertain with the need to accomplish internal goals?

**A:** Original content that can't be found elsewhere is a good way to find a balance. A good storyteller will be able to create compelling content that advances the company and engages the reader. To do this, the blogger needs to have a clear understanding of what resonates with blog readers and then deliver the corporate content in a compelling manner. For example, if you know that videos always get lots of engagement on your blog, post a video interview instead of a written Q&A. Understanding what resonates will help you package the content (that also meets internal goals) in an effective manner.

**Q:** What insights or advice would you give corporate bloggers with regard to creating more engaging and effective posts?

**A:** The key to creating engaging and effective posts is to deliver content that you, the author, would find interesting. You are often your toughest critic, and if you're engaged with your writing, chances are the reader will feel the same. We find that original content is key. For example, if you are writing about a new product introduction, don't just repost a press release – use the blog as a vehicle to provide new content (video, podcast, photos) that build on your company's announcement. Engage your readers for that direct feedback you can't get by sending a release over the wire.

**Q:** Corporate blogs often allow comments, but how do you really make sure customers feel like they have a voice in the conversation, and that it's being heard?

**A:** If your blog allows comments, a good way to ensure customers feel heard is to answer questions that are posted in the comments section. This is important to not only ensure that they feel heard, but also to encourage the dialogue that a blog fosters.

**Q:** What's the best way to solicit fan or customer feedback?

**A:** Give your readers/fans a reason to engage with you. At the end of most of our blog posts, we have a call to action for readers – asking them to share their opinions or stories about the topic in the comments section. Don't just Tweet "Like us on Facebook and follow us on Twitter!" — give them a reason to do so.

---

## MAKE SOCIAL MEDIA ABOUT YOUR CUSTOMERS

Laura, "@Pistachio" Fitton, inbound marketing evangelist for HubSpot, believes that now, more than ever, social media is all about the customer. If your company's social media efforts aren't focused on end-users, then your company and your brand won't grow. Following, she provides answers to the most common questions on how to be a better social media participant.

**Q:** How do you successfully define a brand through social media?

**A:** Take whatever you are doing now, and simply turn it inside out so that it is MUCH more about the audience than it is about your company or brand. The style consider-ations can be the same, but the targeting has to put the question of "Is this useful to our audience?" front and center. If it's not useful, you won't get the audience.

**Q:** Should your company create individual personalities to serve as voices within social media that are separate from corporate channels?

**A:** Yes, if you have the right talent to do so. They have to be comfortable with the media platform, and they have to put some energy into it.

**Q:** What are some of the most common mistakes corporations make with regard to social media and social communications?

**A:** Not investing enough time in the listen and research phase, so that their initial debut on the platform is selfish and tone deaf. I tell audiences to "Listen. Learn. Care. Serve." That means listen for a while, first get the flow of the conversation, the local dialects, the topics of interest, and then learn from that and earnestly care if what you're putting out there is a fit. It's a lot like working the room at a cocktail party, actually. Don't go in bragging and pitching.

**Q:** What are the most frequent mistakes corporations make with regard to social media and crisis situations, and what would be a better way to use these channels or respond?

**A:** Silence is probably number one, followed closely by defensiveness or prickliness. In a true crisis, it is far better to publish a message along the lines of "We don't know, but we are working on it," immediately than to wait 20 minutes or three hours for a perfect response.

**Q:** Who in the organization should contribute to social media accounts to make sure they most resonate with the public? Individuals from throughout the company or a dedicated internal social media team?

**A:** Both are the best possible way to go. Have a dedicated team, but plug that team into the fabric of your company in such a way that they can quickly access the answers, voices and experts they need to manage a situation. It's also great when you have a situation like HubSpot, where many of our top executives are extremely engaged on social media. Our top brass are incredibly engaged on Twitter, and it makes the company so much more human and accountable.

**Q:** How should you deal with negative commentary via social media channels?

**A:** Graciously, no matter how egregious. Some of the most valuable social capital is earned by dealing fairly and humanely with someone who is not being fair or kind to you. That said, don't be a pushover. Immediately offer candid answers and a private way to connect to discuss it further. Even if your immediate answer is "we don't know," that's better than silence.

**Q:** How do you deal with posts that shouldn't have gone out?

**A:** Own up to it. KitchenAid just had a terrible experience with this, where someone with access to the account misposted a negative, rude, personal political tweet under the @KitchenAid brand. They were swift in acknowledging, apologizing and explaining how they would make it right. Since they responded so quickly and since it was pretty obvious what had happened in the first place, I doubt it's really going to hurt them much, if at all.

**Q:** How should you measure the results of social media participation?

**A:** Fine tune your message with the consideration of the specific platform and the measurement of your results in mind. Every audience and every platform will be a little different. People following a celebrity want a lot more detail than someone following the local bakery. Your best bet is to assume that etiquette equals effectiveness. If your account is ineffective — not yielding audience growth, engagement, clickthroughs, conversation — you're probably doing it too much or too little. Vary it and measure what works better.

**Q:** Many organizations are still coming to grips with social media and the role it plays — what advice would you give them for making sure they use it in a way that's helpful, respectful and useful to both the general public and their brand?

**A:** Make sure they're being helpful, respectful and useful to the kinds of people they want to reach. :-) No, seriously, what we say at HubSpot is: Make Marketing People Love. Really invest the time in producing quality that adds to someone's day or helps them solve a problem. A good litmus test is to ask yourself if someone would want to "pay" to receive what you're publishing — e.g. does it have any real value to anyone other than you?

If people share, repeat, like or repost what you're posting, there's a good chance you're doing it well. As an unexpected example, I set up my Twitter account to automatically share certain HubSpot job posts from our Jobvite software. I worried at first that people would be sick of hearing about HubSpot. As it turns out, nearly every job post @Pistachio has ever tweeted has been retweeted, often multiple times. People need jobs and it's human nature to want to help people find employment.

**Q:** How can we make sure the social media messages we're creating are respectful and productive ones?

**A:** Listen a lot, pay earnest compliments and try to make it much more about them than it is about you.

# Social Media Management

It's free to join services like Facebook, Twitter and Blogspot, and not only is this tempting to those who want to feature their latest products - it's also tempting for those who want to share their expertise, authority and viewpoints. Many companies have therefore jumped on the bandwagon, but before doing so yourself, it's important to allocate adequate research and planning. Just as your grandparents may have once said, there's always a price tag involved, even if the initial purchase doesn't require the spending of cash. For corporations, this can mean added expenditure in terms of time and training for personnel, as well as other, more direct expenditures in terms of content creation, or channel maintenance and upkeep. While joining is free, achieve a high-quality presence on social media sites requires extensive time, commitment and skill. Here are several things to bear in mind that can help you better manage your company's social media participation:

**Understand the Resources and Commitments Involved.**
- Effective social media management is often a full-time job: Customers will expect dialogue not only to flow both ways, but also be timely and frequent – allocate resources, time and manpower accordingly. Some businesses may only be able to participate part-time for professional or financial reasons, however: In this case, note that if you have an employee or employees tweeting or posting updates to Facebook, it's time that they're unable to devote to other tasks – be sure to schedule accordingly. Ultimately, maintaining consistent, running conversation is key, as is regularly making note of and responding to incoming dialogue.
- As alluded above, properly utilizing social media necessitates consistent and frequent commentary, and the use of postings which reinforce your expertise and professional image. Figure out what level of response (and response time) works best for your business and commit to it, allocating time and resources accordingly. Customers may be understandably perplexed if you disappear for any length of time or stop responding to posts.
- Corporate posts do not have to be made by the same individual every time, or an officer of the organization – however, all should maintain a consistent personality, tone and level of value creation. Always be thinking of how you can contribute positively to public dialogue, and add information or insights of worth to readers. In every case, be sure that all representatives of your organization who do post be courteous, respectful and customer-focused, as well as cognizant of brand and style guidelines.

**Don't Spread Yourself or Employees Too Thin**
- An effective social media manager takes time every day to update a business'

presence on all of the social media platforms in which it participates: Have you checked in with your fans, friends or followers today? Creating community and running dialogue requires a running commitment – understand the responsibilities you're taking on before diving into a platform and making a halfhearted stab at user engagement.

• Before launching any social media campaign or presence, make a detailed study of the sites, platforms and services where your desired audience can be found, and that best align with your business' long-term goals and objectives. Focusing attention and presence on these sites will help you maximize outreach efforts and user engagement (and use time and resources most wisely), rather than causing you to be spread thin and participate less effectively across a wider range of vehicles. Frequency and reach are basic marketing principles, as is audience targeting: Concentrating your aim makes it easier to hit your target than employing a shotgun strategy.

• Make sure you or your employees have allocated and scheduled enough workday time to respond and engage within various social media communities. If you can't post content or respond to incoming queries in a timely manner, your fans or customers may come to believe that you aren't listening to them. Not responding to a tweet or a Facebook post can be seen by some as the equivalent of not returning a phone call or email – and while you can't always address all, you can at least make efforts to speak to larger trending topics in public forums, helping assuage the broader user community's concerns.

### Don't Cut and Paste Efforts Across Different Platforms

• Each social network has its own features, personality and community: Study the outlets you participate in, and understand the different nuances so that your message is not simply carbon-copied across each forum in the exact same way. Audiences differ, as do consumption models across social media vehicles: A one-size approach won't work here.

• While social vehicles may vary, make sure your message and brand are consistent and cross-promoted across channels: Establishing a style guide and dedicated social team or member can be tremendously helpful to helping maintain consistency of tone, image and overall user impression and takeaway.

• Figure out who your target audience is, where they exist online and how to best reach them, then target your messages, content and posting frequency accordingly.

### Providing Engaging Info and Adds Value to Conversations

• The more compelling and meaningful your content, the more your customers will engage with it. The key question to ask yourself at every turn: "What's in it for them?"

• Encourage people to communicate, comment and interact with you: One example might include placing a call to action (i.e. a request for viewers' thoughts and feedback) at the bottom of every post. Incentivization is key here – think about the action steps you want readers or viewers to take, and what would drive users to take them.

• Create a two-way conversation that encourages your customers to want to help you promote your message. Simply blasting information out to them is less effective than soliciting their commentary and input.

### Realize that Social Media Means More Than Sharing Ads or Press Releases

• While you can promote your brand and your products on social media services, overtly doing so is often ill-received: Consider finding ways to create benefit for end-users when doing so ("What's your business etiquette IQ – find out in our new online survey!"), and adopt a tone that's less self-promotional.

• People look to social media channels to enjoy a more personalized and social experience. Look for ways to provide such content. Note that many corporations have found success by providing original news, updates on exclusive steals and deals, access to crowdsourced initiatives (submit your best designs –winners will appear in our new national ad campaign!) and behind-the-scenes looks at new products and promotions.

• Expect customers to respond to any and all outreach – and that you'll be expected to engage with them in order to show respect and further the conversation. There's a reason they call it "social" media, after all.

### Be Helpful to Your Audience and Strive to Better Their Condition

• Listen to your audience to discover its likes, needs and interests, then provide insights and information to match. The more you help customers, the more they'll become advocates.

• Loyal and passionate customers should be responded to and engaged with – finding ways to reward and spotlight your community is vitally important. The more you extend the hand of friendship to end-users, and acknowledge their efforts, the bigger fans they'll become, and more goodwill you have the opportunity to generate. The key: To always be up-front and genuine with your audience, and afford them the same respect and standing that they afford your business and brand.

• Be a good resource. Make sure your content is useful and informative, and give visitors tips, links to helpful articles and sites, and other pertinent information. Likewise, don't be afraid to shout out or partner with outside organizations, individuals and influencers who share common philosophies and interests – win-win is always the way to go.

- Always make sure your content and outreach initiatives are relevant to, and create worth for, your customers – this necessitates looking at promotional efforts from new angles, so that the focus is on them, not you.

**Measure Reactions and Respond in Kind**

- If you aren't measuring audience response, it's hard to know whether content is resonating, or who's listening – as a courtesy to your audience, take the time to understand them and build or adapt content strategy to match.
- If social media campaigns or individual aspects of them aren't working, don't be afraid to change and tweak them – the best outreach efforts are constantly being updated, refined and optimized in real-time.
- Understand who your industry influencers – those capable of prompting others' actions and provoking change – are, and how to best engage with them. All operate via different platforms and channels, speak to different audiences, and have differing objectives and goals. Look at how these individuals are interpreting and responding to your messaging, and speak with them to adapt to better serve both they and their audiences' needs.

## SOCIAL MARKETING: FINDING YOUR CORPORATE VOICE

Mary Renouf, director of social marketing at T-Mobile, engages with customers across the spectrum, and possesses intimate knowledge of just what it takes to develop a successful presence on social media sites. Here are her favorite tips on establish and evolving an engaging personality for your brand across online communications channels:

**Q:** How do you create a compelling corporate voice on social media accounts without sounding unprofessional?

**A:** For my brand, I focus on making sure that every message we post checks off some of our key criteria. Is it fun and imaginative? Is it energetic and enthusiastic? Does it draw attention with cool and exciting details? Your tone drives how the consumer interacts with you. Speak to them as individuals, in a way that everyone understands.

**Q:** How do you create engaging content with regard to social media channels that users will want to seek out and share?

**A:** My goal is always to make sure the content is inviting, interactive and accessible. We ask lots of questions, we reference popular culture, and most importantly, we deliver small, bite-size content frequently. I think the biggest thing you can do is encourage people to interact with you – ask them to share the news, start a debate and keep it fresh, and never ignore a conversation they start with you. If you're engaging with your consumers frequently, they will be receptive to your posts that clearly have a brand objective. Creating a two-way communications strategy actually drives your consumers to want to help you push out your message is crucial. They want to hear things from you first, so they will often seek out the brand page to get information – therefore accomplishing internal initiatives.

**Q:** How do brands figure in with social marketing personality and tone of voice, as businesses typically have stringent corporate guidelines?

**A:** Always know your tone of voice, always know your Rules of Engagement, and make sure your posts stick to that. Have a standard messaging cadence and make sure you supervise it – it can always be modified if you're keeping tabs on how well it's working. Social marketing campaigns are based on the idea that you are continuously optimizing – and oftentimes on the fly. You never know when a specific piece of content will land you a trending topic or one of your highest engagement rates ever – but be prepared to capitalize on it. Have a second post with further information ready to go – re-tweet or share a specific post from a consumer that further legitimizes your post.

**Q:** Should the same corporate personality presented in other mediums be the same you present in social media?

**A:** I think people tend to expect a slightly different tone on social mediums. This is where they are most comfortable engaging with you – so you have to be prepared to engage back. If you have standard replies for common questions, that's fine. But you also have to be prepared for the next question. If you're willing to engage with a consumer, you have to be willing to engage to a point where they leave the community having a good experience. And most importantly, social is a great place to "be real" – this is where your fans can tolerate a typo, and they understand your app might not work 100% of the time. You always strive for perfection, but if ever there was a customer who is ready to take you as you are – that's your social consumer.

**Q:** What are some of the most common mistakes corporations make with regard to social media and social communications?

**A:** The most common mistakes are too frequent communications, too few communications or too "branded" communications. Finding the cadence that works well for your brand and your consumers is key. Some brands can post all day long, and their fans want to hear from them. Other brands have little value in posts that occur more than once a week. It's a fine balance and it takes some practice: Ultimately, I think brands need to be more willing to test the waters.

Another common mistake is thinking that everyone of your fans is coming to your page every day, or following every tweet you make. You have to look at social as if it's Grand Central Station – you can stand in the middle and yell, and people who are interested in what you say might stop and listen, others are going to pass you by, some will be annoyed and others will stop and participate. You have to account for that when you plan your messaging. Make it bite-size, make it interesting and make it relevant.

**Q:** How do you make sure every customer has a voice in the conversation when engaging in social dialogue?

**A:** Be prepared to address questions, comments and concerns. Be responsive, don't wait a week before you answer. Be sure to address people in your responses if they've asked a very specific question. Even if the best you can do is to direct them to a customer support person, at least you've acknowledged them and made them feel as though they were heard.

Another great tactic for brands is to create an ambassador program. Find those people who are engaging with your brand frequently, those that have a clear passion for your company. Reward them by giving them information first, allowing them to test your new products and letting them provide input into your campaign. Then ask them to help answer questions they see on the page and have them serve as advisors to new fans. Just make sure they identify themselves as ambassadors and not employees.

**Q:** What are the most frequent mistakes corporations make with regard to social media crisis situations, and what would be a better way to use these channels or respond?

**A:** The first mistake is in not having a crisis management policy. Without that, you don't know how to respond, how quickly to respond, how frequently to respond and what your follow-up process is. Set a plan and make sure legal, PR, business operations, marketing and all other key stakeholders sign-off. Have contacts for these situations. Nobody wants to have to deal with a crisis, but being prepared for it always makes it easier.

Another mistake is in assuming that your entire community knows about your crisis. If you're going to respond to an incident, make sure you are clear about what the incident is and how people can learn more. A lot of people who follow you may have no idea what's going on with your brand, so your communications must be clear at every level of the crisis management plan.

**Q:** What are your top rules for social media success?

1.  Surprise and delight – spontaneously reward your engaged fans.
2.  Police any 'bullying' between fans on a social media channel.
3.  Don't ignore conversations.
4.  Be the first to break news (but break it even if you're not).

# MARKETING, PUBLIC RELATIONS AND SOCIAL CAMPAIGNS

The role of marketing and public relations within professional organizations has shifted drastically with the advent of social media, and move to greater emphasis on storytelling. Traditionally, organizations would simply broadcast news, or channel it through one specific type of influencer – members of the media – and observe the reaction, then respond on a somewhat more flexible timetable. Today, it's not simply about beaming out a message: It's about building trust with end-users, telling a compelling story and creating social streams of dialogue that work two ways.

In a connected, online and multitasking world, companies must first find ways to connect with increasingly fragmented audiences, then work to build empathy and awareness, and create channels through which customers and influencers of every sort can engage with brands and products in exciting new ways. Moreover, customer impression carries increasing weight, with brand impression able to travel greater distances in less time than ever before, and users growingly looking to their personal networks for expertise and validation as opposed to traditional media channels. However, while the media matrix and consumption patterns have irrevocably shifted, the value of powerful communication strategies has only become more vital. In fact, traditional marketing and public relations principles play more of a role than ever, and practitioners can excel in the modern world – provided, that is, they adapt to changing markets and best practices. Following are several key areas to keep in mind as you work to create and nurture positive conversation.

## Email and Online Marketing: Best Practices
- Ask permission from recipients first before adding them to mailing lists. Permission-based marketing is the law, not just proper etiquette.
- Resist the temptation to spam your list by mailing at well spaced out intervals: There's a fine line between being consistent with sending email messages and overdoing it. Test to determine your optimal email frequency.
- Balance automated messages with non-automated messages to make exchanges feel more personal.
- Make it easy for recipients to unsubscribe with a single click – they should not be required to enter their email address again, specifying reasons for doing so, or otherwise take further action. Do not mail them a confirmation email that they have been unsubscribed – state that requests to be removed from lists are successful in the same browser window where requests are processed right after the click.

- If someone asks to be unsubscribed from your list, honor their request, no questions asked.
- Scrub your list of subscribers regularly to ensure that you're delivering email to the right address, and minimizing possible email bouncebacks.
- Touch base – gently, professionally and kindly – with subscribers who've lapsed or not interacted with you lately. If they're no longer engaged, a gentle probe can show that you care. Ask if they'd like to unsubscribe or would prefer to receive different forms of contact or emails at a differing frequency.
- Personalize mailings and address them as you would when conversing with real people – not just a faceless horde.
- Be certain that any automated fields – e.g. those that insert first names ("Hi Mary!") – do not show these names in different colors, fonts or trappings from the rest of the email, otherwise you risk running the gaffe of revealing that it's a mass mailing.
- Segment your emails. Divide your database into different groups, interest types and audience members to more accurately target your marketing efforts and better resonate with recipients.
- Make sure any 'reply to' fields go to a real person, not your own spam filter!
- Make sure your emails are mobile device friendly. Many recipients read these missives on smartphones, tablets and other portable gadgets.
- Remove spam triggers to the best of your ability, and be clear about where any and all links contained in an email lead.
- Do not misrepresent the content of emails or links either, or be misleading with titles and queries.

**Proper Press and Media Outreach**
- Make sure you're sending your press releases, emails and marketing materials to journalists and members of the media who actually cover the topic that you are promoting.
- Be sure to target the specific editor of the section or area of the publication you're looking to reach.
- If you're not sure if someone is interested in receiving your information, don't be afraid to try the old-fashioned route: Place a phone call and ask them, or drop a note, before adding them to mass mailing lists.
- Be polite, be professional and know when to back off. If a reporter isn't interested, don't take it personally, and don't spam his or her inbox.
- Be timely: If a member of the media makes an inquiry while he or she is working on deadline, jump on it and be as helpful as you can. Oftentimes, the PR professional who gets back to a reporter on deadline the fastest gets the best placement in a story, and enjoys a better measure of trust from the journalist going forward as a reliable source.

- Likewise, do not promise access to contacts, information or material that you cannot deliver, or cannot be delivered by the necessary deadline: All it takes is one blown promise to undermine one's trust and credibility.
- Do not ask to see the story or video before it goes public – this is highly inappropriate, and a severe breach of trust.
- Do make sure your press releases are polished. You never know if a writer or editor will publish what you've wrote verbatim.
- When following up, be respectful of a journalist's time and interest, and attempt to contact them in total no more than two to three times.
- Be aware of publications' various lead times. Know that most printed works have long lead times that may extend 90 to 120 days into the future. Ex: A press release about an event happening next month that is sent to a publication that files its content four months in advance is an exercise in futility.
- Know that writers and reporters aren't the ultimate gatekeepers. If their editor doesn't clear a story, or decides for whatever reason it cannot make print (even for unexpected lack of space in the section due to lowered ad count), it won't run.
- If a journalist makes a mistake, be polite in requesting a retraction or a correction.
- Don't be afraid to ask a reporter what he or she is working on next: You might be able to help with another story or feature.

## Corporate News and Announcements

- When you send a press release to groups of contacts, make sure to BCC them, so you are not exposing all other journalists' email addresses to random strangers.
- If it is an important announcement, be clear about any specifics, including embargoes.
- If you negotiate an exclusive deal with a journalist, be certain to specify all specifics up-front to avoid later issues or concerns – e.g. is it a print exclusive, online, based upon a certain time window, etc? Do not promise an exclusive if you cannot deliver.
- Respect publications' editorial calendars and lead times when pitching – many are publicly available for reference, which can help you optimize pitch timing and angles.
- Once you issue a press release, be responsive to interested journalists and members of the media. Be available to answer all questions, conduct interviews and provide access to necessary information, parties or assets.

## Content Marketing and Bylined Articles

- Do your homework: When pitching bylined or sponsored content, target only those publications and websites that accept these forms of material.
- Similarly, only pitch op-eds or pieces from corporate or market insiders to those outlets which accept guests posts, and respect their guidelines for submissions, which

are often posted publicly for review.

• Make sure that any guest bloggers or writers submitted fit the subject matter, tone and writing style of the publication, and that any submissions are professionally written and edited before being turned in to these outlets.

• Study any targeted publications and websites before pitching to make an appropriately tailored and individualized pitch.

• Rather than spam random editors, find out who the best contact person is and specific target pitch efforts at this individual.

• Conduct research up-front to determine if your company will need to pay for having content placed or articles run in the specific outlet – it can save a lot of wasted time and energy, and save you from garnering spurned recipients' ill-will.

• Always approach publications respectfully and with an eye towards providing content that readers will appreciate, enjoy and find value in.

• Be subtle with sales efforts – make sure your biography includes appropriate links and pertinent information about you and your business, but do not make overt promotional pitches throughout the piece, or seek to belittle competitors.

**Crystallizing and Communicating a Clear Corporate Social Media Policy**

• Make it clear to employees what is okay to share online and what isn't, how and when to do so, and the most appropriate manner in which to conduct outreach efforts. With every employee a brand ambassador, training should begin the first day on the job to reinforce and instill the importance of these corporate values – establishing formal rules of engagement, clearly communicating them to workers, and explaining what's expected from hires is crucial.

• Guidelines are only the beginning, however: Establish an internal program designed to teach social media literacy and aptitude, provide continued education efforts, and reward employees for successfully practicing these skills – you may wish to consider regular skills refreshes, training sessions, certification courses, and gamification-based programs to reinforce these maxims.

• Social media training should include real-world, hands-on examples in practice (e.g. by allowing employees to participate in sample exchanges over internal corporate networks), and built to promote education and empowerment. Employees won't just be sharing updates from the front lines or breaking announcements, but also insights, information and opinions as part of social efforts, and must possess the wherewithal to do so smartly and professionally.

• Establish and promote key values amongst employees who'll engage in social media efforts to help guide their decision-making process – understanding the importance of integrity, moderation, gratitude, self-control and other virtues can help guide their efforts going forward.

- Be straightforward and specific about what's expected in terms of tone, attitude, end-results and output from your social media pros, and regularly monitor and assess how we'll they're aligning with and meeting these goals. Providing running feedback and commentary to help them grow and improve is a vital way to bolster performance in these areas. To this extent, you may wish to have team leaders provide sample tweets, posts or updates to provide a sense of how to better shape these communications efforts.
- For sake of clarity and assurance of appropriate conduct, also post formal guidelines for communication within your own blogs, communities and online venues, public-facing or otherwise. Having established guidelines in place helps set expectations up-front, provide level playing field, and help you address any issues that may arise, such as having to ban argumentative users or remove inappropriate posts.

**Disclaimers and Warranties**
- As many employees mention their job title and employer in their social media profiles, you may wish to encourage them to place a disclaimer such as "opinions are my own" on their profile description – e.g. on Twitter, having it read "Social Media Marketer and PR Maven for Acme Corp. Dog lover. Passionate About Dancing and Yoga. Opinions are My Own."
- When employees make official corporate posts, or to help promote initiatives, you may wish to have them preface thoughts by saying "Donating my status to [company name goes here]."
- Put formal communications, privacy and legal policies in place including appropriate disclaimers and warranties on all public- and internal-facing channels, and make it obvious and clear at the time of signup or registration what specific policies are in place for users of corporate channels, communities and websites should they choose to utilize these solutions.

**Setting Clear Guidelines for Consumer Interaction**
- The immediacy of social media allows you to interact with your business' customers directly and often without filters – however, policy and protocols must be set in place beforehand to ensure professional and productive interactions. Understanding the some room must be given to operate between formal guidelines, make it clear to employees what appropriate rules of conduct are when speaking directly to end-users or customers, whether exchanges are B2B or B2C in nature.
- Provide ongoing development and training regarding these policies, and make sure employees who manage social media efforts, outreach and campaigns receive regular, ongoing instruction – and are passing learning and knowledge gained from direct frontline interactions with customers on throughout the organization to promote

positive transfer and enhance best practices. Creating internal sharing systems, online platforms and programs where employees can share insights, ask questions and contribute individual findings can greatly assist in this regard – sharing findings, knowledge and commentary on the back of ongoing efforts helps boost program growth, engagement and participation.

- Marketing campaigns and branding efforts should also adhere to consistent guidelines, helping you ensure the right messages are being sent and that your company is being portrayed with the image and professionalism you desire.
- Outside of formal guidelines, basic rules of politeness, professionalism and business etiquette should be practiced online, just as you would when engaging with a customer face-to-face.
- Through social media, you will likely also interact not just with individual customers, but entire communities of customers who follow certain blogs, trends, etc. Identify which influencers to reach out to, the best methods for doing so, and optimum means of engaging them, and ensure employees are briefed on these topics – as in real-life, virtual group dynamics can differ greatly from one-on-one interactions.
- Casual is fine in social media exchanges, disrespectful is not. While it's OK to keep things fun and light (when discussing appropriate topics) online, organizations must still treat customers with the utmost care, concern and professionalism – let real-life interactions be your guideline.
- Across customers and fans, you will discover superfans and influencers: Among the most highly-desired and –courted of all social media audiences – be certain to afford all heightened levels of respect and attention, and prioritize these exchanges. Influencers and experts in your field who tout your business or corporation may command greater levels of dedicated time and attention from staff – providing it is a sign of mutual respect for the time and attention they pay you. However, good rule of thumb when it comes to social media and customer service is always "spoil everybody" – practice it, and you'll be in good shape no matter whom you're interacting with.
- When making outreach to influencers – professionals, experts, media, community leaders, thought leaders or otherwise – understand that optimum methods for contacting each differ between individuals.

Depending on your business and social media strategy, consider the platforms and topics all are most active around, and optimum solutions for making targeted outreach based on this learning.

**Putting Crisis Plans in Place and Promoting Rapid Response Times**
- As soon as a crisis hits, the key is to get ahead of it. Ground the conversation. Don't be unreachable or leaving audiences hanging, the virtual equivalent of allowing uncomfortable pauses to appear in dialogue – be present, even if the only answer you

have temporarily is "we're working on finding out the answer now."

- Be present, be transparent and be human.
- If you've made a mistake, take responsibility and fix it.
- If you don't know, say you don't know immediately, and that you're looking into it.
- A successful social media manager takes time every day to monitor chatter surrounding a brand and update a business's presence on all of the social media platforms in which it participates. He or she should know about a crisis as or immediately after it happens and respond quickly and appropriately. Take time to monitor and review channels, including conversation as it coalesces around your business and related topics.

## Promoting Messages Across Different Mediums

- When you've got a good story to tell, it often makes sense to tell it across multiple mediums to maximize your reach – but tailor content and promotions by platform. The way individuals consume content on Twitter is very different from that of Facebook or Pinterest. A one-size-fits-all approached is not advised: However, if you've got a YouTube video containing several fun or juicy nuggets of information, the incremental effort to write a blog post, schedule some tweets featuring highlights, or otherwise adapt it for use in other formats can easily be justified.
- As alluded, tailor your message according to the medium to best resonate with and serve your audience: Content can take myriad short- or long-form shapes – all of which should be adapted for the platform, and easy user consumption. Remember, each medium has its strengths and weaknesses. Visual promotions such as infographics might best be served on Pinterest, Facebook and Google+, while key points from them might be better called out in short spurts on Twitter.
- Bring value to online conversations by looking for ways to add unique information and insights, and acknowledge and respond to others' reactions.
- Always be respectful when interacting with others online, and keep a cool head, even when you encounter rude or inappropriate behavior by other parties.
- Be helpful to others, and find ways through your comments, content and actions to create value and benefit for recipients. Doing a good turn for colleagues, customers and others we interact with across different forms of media helps promote goodwill and empathy – valuable business assets.

## Expressing Your Brand's Personality

- When people go to social media sites, they expect exchanges to be more personal, more immediate and more engaging: Be less formal, but make sure you adhere to the rules and guidelines your company sets forth about your brand, message and tone of voice while also creating value for your audience.

- Casual and fun doesn't equate to flippant, glib or self-centered – think about how you or your brand may be perceived, and take care to present yourself as affably and respectfully as possible. Be cognizant of post quality as well, including taking care to eliminate grammatical and spelling errors. Note that kindness, courtesy, positivity and empathy should be reflected in every post.
- Humor is appropriate to use depending on context – however, only the same sort of humor that is appropriate for use in an office or business casual setting. Avoid risqué or controversial statements.

## SOCIAL MEDIA AND MARKETING: BRIDGING THE GAP

Just about every corporation has a voice on Twitter, a Facebook page and even an official blog. Not every company, however, utilizes these social media tools well, and some companies do so much more adroitly than others. Because of the medium's growingly prominent role in business, we turned to Jamie Grenney, vice president of video and social media for Salesforce.com, for expert advice and insight.

**Q:** Information has the power to travel further and faster than ever before – and marketing dialogue suddenly works both ways. How can we truly make customers feel like their opinions are voices are being listened and responded to?

**A:** Every company should be thinking about rolling out a listening and engagement playbook. Using tools like the Marketing Cloud so you can track every one of your brand mentions across social channels and make sure you're engaging in the right way is important. You might want to jump in to thank an advocate or help address the needs of someone who is frustrated. Salesforce.com also has a program called the IdeaExchange. If our customers have feedback about our products or services, we encourage them post their idea there. So far we've generated over 29,000 ideas. By tracking each one and showing which ones we've delivered on, it builds up a tremendous amount of goodwill. The important takeaway: You need to listen to your customers, engage where they are, and show that you have taken action on their ideas and feedback.

**Q:** How can marketing, social media and PR professionals best work together as a team?

**A:** For starters, I think it's valuable for campaigns for the social team and PR team to sit close together, because there is a lot of overlap and shared resources. We need to think about how we use traditional tactics, plus our social plays, to drive the incremental pipeline. And we need to think about how we use influencers and our social channels to amplify our reach.

**Q:** What's the ultimate goal: More likes, tweets, shares, stories? Or is there a better metric for gauging effectiveness of campaigns?

**A:** Our social media metrics include the number of subscribers, the number of blog visits, video views, and shares of conversation. But more and more, it is about tying social media to your pipeline. With the birth of the social customer profile, we can start to tie social media with campaign influenced-media. We also need to develop plays for driving the pipeline directly from social channels, the same way as we have a playbook for email marketing or search marketing.

**Q:** Today, more and more of us – including businesses, brands and professionals – find ourselves in the relationship business, whether with buyers, the media, everyday fans, etc. How can we make sure we're creating respectful and productive ones?

**A:** That's the marriage of customer relationship management (CRM) and Social. We need to understand the conversations that are taking place, who is influential, who's on top of it, and what the business impact of these exchanges are. That'll allow us to provide outstanding customer service and grow relationships.

## THE FUTURE OF PUBLIC RELATIONS

Frank Strong, director of public relations for Vocus and PRWeb, knows that while the mediums have changed, the messengers may in many cases still be scrambling to play catch-up. Happily, there are many ways that public relations professionals can re-adapt for life at the speed of the Internet, and excel in both online and social media markets. He offers advice and tips on how to improve your company's PR efforts with regard to high-tech communications.

**Q:** How has public relations changed in the age of the Internet and social media?

**A:** Every organization is now a media company. This has created an opportunity for businesses to develop their own community and following. A brand is now able to earn media when the traction of its own publishing crosses a threshold that's too large to ignore.

**Q:** What's the best way to promote your business in social media?

**A:** Traditional PR principles are still valid in social media. In fact, PR's background in working with editorial contacts is one of the reasons I believe that public relations can naturally excel in a social world. "Markets are conversations," according to the Cluetrain Manifesto, written more than a decade ago, and that's what public relations is all about. The single best way to capture attention is to have a compelling idea and share it with the right audience at the right time. This was true for PR ten years ago, and it's still true today.

**Q:** Customers (including everyone we interact with – fans, media, etc. – not just those who buy from us) have more of a voice in any conversation than ever: What's the proper way to engage with them and make sure their opinions are respected and heard?

**A:** We should encourage customer viewpoints, foster them and actively respond. The biggest mistakes I see are 1) Organizations don't respond at all, when everyone wants to be acknowledged or 2) Shying from constructive criticism. Look at the reviews on some of the most popular review sites: Many of them are entirely positive – and when too positive, that leads to cynicism. A few points that are constructively critical won't hurt – in fact, it's more believable.

**Q:** What tone of voice and degree of personality are now appropriate in online marketing?

**A:** I think a more informal tone and personality has to be more appropriate because we have more voices in the mix: Just marketing or just PR isn't the sole owner of communications anymore – all organizations have employees that can contribute to the discussion. The organizations that have really cracked the code on content marketing have actively encouraged their employees to contribute, and there has to be an acceptance that not every discussion will have the polish of an accomplished writer or producer. And that's okay because they are still able to connect with their communities and are probably using a language and choice of words that better fits that community.

**Q:** How can corporations who want to maintain control of their brands still engage the public via social media in productive ways?

**A:** We have to recognize that unanticipated directions can lead to new opportunities – this is especially true if it's our customers making the statement. But this idea isn't new, as we've seen it over and over with product development. A new technology emerges, and then customers start using it in a way that wasn't anticipated. Remember 3M's PostIt Note story? That was supposed to be a bookmark that evolved into a best-selling product because the inventor watched and observed what people were doing with it. The same can be true with communications – customers will better identify with companies that speak their language.

## PLANNING YOUR SOCIAL MEDIA STRATEGY

The customer is always right: An adage always worth remembering, but now, with the advent of social media, one worth keeping in mind more than ever, as customers can share their opinion faster and with more peers than ever before. How can you best handle the complex interplay of customer engagement, and customer service, that now takes place over social media? Katie Wagner, president of Katie Wagner Social Media, offers some adept strategies.

**Q:** In an era of more informed consumers and increasingly hard to reach target markets, what's the best way to capture customer and media attention in a compelling way?

**A:** Traditional marketing is changing. Social media has made storytelling more important than ever – building an emotional connection with your target audience. Every marketer has to be a journalist of sorts, finding the stories behind what their brand or business does every day, and telling them in a way that engages and builds credibility. Good stories contain people, and anecdotal evidence is more important than ever. Stats aren't as compelling as they once were – consumers want to feel something for your brand.

The other change that factors in is that increasingly, people want to find their own information. They want to be able to Google a topic, read about it, and feel as if they are coming to their own conclusion. They want to make their own decisions – without being 'sold' to. This is one of the things that makes social media so powerful for consumers: It gives them a whole new layer of research. As business owners, then, our job is to put content out there for them to find. Not just on our websites, but in the form of blog posts, videos, white papers, webinars... content that educates and informs, but never sells. We want to help our customers to be the best possible consumers of our industries, without ever asking them directly to choose us.

This type of marketing engages in ways that traditional 'promotions' can't. It builds us up as experts, keeps us front and center, but ultimately lets the consumer comes to the decision on their own terms.

**Q:** Many organizations are still coming to grips with social media and the role it plays – what advice would you give them for making sure they use it in a way that's helpful, respectful and useful to both the general public and their brand?

**A:** Social media is not a medium to jump into lightly. Just as with any other corporate communication strategy, it must be well thought through before deployment. This is not a place for 'winging it' or ad libbing. Even inside a brand that has a more relaxed and conversational style, the topics and composition of posts should be well-planned. It's important to implement a strategy that includes:

1. What channels will you use, and why?
2. How will you ensure that the voice is consistent across all communications?
3. What is your brand's voice?
4. What will you do if a problem arises?
5. What is your ultimate goal for social media?
6. How will you measure that goal?

I always advise brands to start small. Rolling out a new social media initiative does not mean you have to have a presence on every channel. Start with one or two channels that you feel most comfortable with. Do them well. Measure your results. When you're ready, you can expand.

This medium is also part of a long-term marketing plan. Social media is not ever 'finished,' and it takes time to build and generate activity. Don't begin unless you plan to put the time and resources in over a period of six months to a year, before gauging its effectiveness.

**Q:** Social media accounts – should we stick to one main one, or is it more appropriate to segment and have different accounts for different services, subsidiaries or categories of products?

**A:** This really depends on the brand. In most cases, I think it's better to have one main corporate channel. However, some very large brands that have products in completely different sectors, all with strong followings, have done well by segmenting the pages. P&G comes to mind. The answer really lies in what kind of resources, human and financial, you have to maintain a social media presence. Creating channels and running them poorly will hurt you more than not having them to begin with. You must be able to sustain anything you create, so make the decision carefully and with a long-term plan in mind.

In the case of retailers, who have many locations, but sell the same products and services in each, I think one online location is best. A main corporate channel can have much better control of the brand's image and with content from many different locations to draw from, a dynamic presence can be created.

For businesses that franchise, this decision becomes more difficult. It may be alright to allow franchisees to create their own presence on social media, but there needs to be some brand standards in place about how the language, logo and layout are used to support the brand. Otherwise, you run the risk of diluting the power of the brand itself.

This is a new medium, and many brands are jumping into it without thinking through what to do with different locations/products/services etc. Since most social media channels issue custom URLs and handles, you run the risk of one 'brand' page taking those names, and leaving another page for the same brand high and dry. Whatever a brand decides to do, a branding strategy should be established from the beginning, so plans can be made accordingly.

**Q:** How can corporations engage with the public in productive fashion, handle situations when messaging takes unexpected directions, and maintain some degree of control over trusted properties without shooting themselves in the foot when situations develop in unanticipated ways?

**A:** The short answer to 'How do you maintain control?' is: You can't. Social media is in many ways an open forum, and by entering the arena, you have to be willing to roll with the punches. The number one rule is that when someone mentions your company – whether it is directed to you or not – you must respond. Turning the other cheek is asking for more trouble, because consumers use a public medium to extract a reply. These days, customers see social media as the most direct line to customer service. If they put a situation out there, they are looking to have it resolved. So you have to respond, but it's always best to take the high road.

Other customers are always watching, so handle the situation in a way that you would be proud to have them see. Be respectful. Be empathetic. And in every situation possible, work to fix the problem. As much as they can, a brand should try to take complaints offline as quickly as possible. If someone writes a tweet or a Yelp review, message them and ask for a number where they can be reached. Have the conversation away from social media if possible, and only return to the public forum once it has been resolved.

In some cases, a resolution may not be possible, and then it may be appropriate for a brand to issue a public statement about the situation. This should be done on the same channel where the complaint was made, and in a short, unemotional 'just the facts' manner. Everyone is entitled to their opinion, and making those opinions public is easier than ever before. The most successful brands on social media are those that choose to take every opportunity to learn about their customers, and further that relationship. Even when the conversation is unexpected, it could be a valuable chance to hear from a segment of your audience that you wouldn't have engaged with otherwise.

**Q:** Customers are beginning to pick up on frivolous exchanges — there's even a "Condescending Corporate Brand Page" satirical page that users can like on Facebook. How can we talk to social media users without coming off as condescending, and truly create value for them and conversations that matter?

**A:** The key to this is good listening skills and authenticity. The more open and authentic a brand is, the more well received they will be in the social realm. Every time you sit down at the keyboard, think of yourself as standing in front of a room full of people who say they're interested in your product or service, but haven't made up their mind to buy yet. Your job is not to convince them, but simply to answer questions, provide information, and continue the conversation.

When we try to "market" or "sell" on social media, we end up failing because consumers see through it. Instead, we must tell our story. We must be likable. And trustworthy. But above all, real. You don't know whether your audience on social media has bought anything — or even will. But you do know they are interested enough to be there to listen, so treat them with respect. And by listening back, a brand can learn valuable lessons about who their potential customers are and what they care about.

It's a cocktail party scenario — if you walked up to someone new and talked only about yourself and what you had to offer, your new acquaintance would quickly look for an excuse to walk away. But if you asked questions and were genuinely interested in the answers, they would be happy talking to you all night. It's the same strategy on social media. The more interested you are in them, the more interesting they will suddenly find you.

**Q:** What's the ultimate goal: More likes, tweets, shares, stories? Or is there a better metric for gauging the effectiveness of campaigns?

**A:** Engagement is always better than sheer numbers. If you have 3,000 'fans' who aren't interacting with the content you're putting out, and are basically just watching you scroll by in a newsfeed or Twitter stream, that won't do much to help your business. On the other hand, if you had 300 fans who thought you were smart and credible, read everything you put out, interacted with the information you were sharing, and passed it along to their friends – that would impact your business in a big way. Engagement (comments, shares, retweets, conversation) keeps you and your business top of mind, so fans remember you when it's time to buy or refer business.

At the end of the day, it strokes our egos to see big numbers, but it's less important how many fans you have, and more important how they feel about you. Growing a community and building that 'know, like and trust' factor will eventually increase your bottom line. And isn't that why we, as business owners, are getting involved in social media? You have to see results.

**Q:** The trick to fostering productive conversation with customers online today is?

**A:** I think it's important to remember that these days, consumers see past a well-written website. They realize that it's information that we want them to know about our businesses – we wrote it. They're demanding to know more about who we really are, because it's so easy to find that information. On your social media channels, you did not write everything that's said about your business, or you as a business owner. With Yelp reviews, LinkedIn recommendations, mentions on Twitter and Facebook wall posts so accessible to our potential customers, we have to be aware that they are getting a much more authentic look at our businesses than they have in the past.

And that must cause a return to good, old-fashioned customer service. You have to treat everyone you interact with as if they are your most important customer, because chances are, many of your most important customers are watching. Every user on social media has the power to sing your praises, or sully your reputation. Clients often ask me if they can delete it when someone makes a negative post about them. The fact is, in some cases you can, but I don't believe you should.

No one believes that we, as business owners, make everyone happy 100% of the time. If all the feedback is glowing, it looks a little fishy. Also, by deleting or ignoring a comment from a customer, you run the risk of making them angrier and escalating the situation. It says a lot more about you as a business or a business owner to have people see you treat that customer with respect. Show concern about the problem, and work to resolve it. The old maxim 'the customer is always right' has never been more true – or more important.

The answer to maintaining good relationships on social media is authenticity. Be real, be honest, be forthcoming - and show genuine concern when someone has a bad experience. People will forgive you for a mistake, but they don't forgive as easily if you sweep it under the rug, or look the other directions. Those things that used to take place behind closed doors are now very much out in the open.

# JOB HUNTING AND CAREERS

Job hunting has evolved beyond simply dropping off paper résumés and occasionally checking the newspaper want ads. Today, it's about registering for recruitment websites, making email introductions through LinkedIn, connecting with colleagues on social channels, and sending virtual portfolios bouncing across the web. But how can you ensure the website or, for that matter, the person on the other will respond in timely fashion, be receptive to your query and is committed to maintaining your professional privacy? There are several new rules of online etiquette to remember when chasing job opportunities smartly and securely.

## General Tips

- Observe the same rules of behavior in online job searches as in real-life — professional conduct, appearances and communications are imperative.
- Proper formalities should be observed when conducting job outreach, and care should be taken to respect the rules of grammar, punctuation and spelling in all communications, whether they take the form of a tweet, blog post or email.
- Be especially careful with regard to how electronic communications may be perceived — tone of voice, expressions and subtle nuances can be lost in the translation to text.
- Include your name and contact information in all communications, using respectful signature rules (as referenced in How to Close Emails and Establishing a Respectable Signature). All personal contact numbers and email addresses should be separate from your current job contact information.
- Always review prospective employers' rules for submission to determine exact material sought and how they prefer that it be sent electronically before submitting résumés and cover letters.
- Résumés should include keywords (specific phrases frequently used to denote job titles and descriptions, professional experience, and technical terms when performing computerized or online queries). You can many times find these keywords (e.g. "systems administrator" vs. "IT expert") in the job description itself. Making false or misleading statements that misrepresent your experience or skill set is unethical, however.
- Be aware that document formatting may not be preserved through all electronic contact methods, and preview all your submissions before sending them. While your résumé may look natty in your word processor, errors including unwanted line breaks, poor formatting and font troubles may appear when entered into email programs or

online contact forms.

- Note that résumés, once sent, may be publicly viewable (including to your current boss) and – if you've custom tailored for multiple submissions – in a multitude of forms.
- All online presences should be professional and reflect an appropriate work image – from personal blogs to social network profiles and photo sharing sites, assume that all will be visible to prospective employers.
- Be advised that job searches conducted on work devices and computers may be visible to your current employer.

## Creating a Positive Personal Brand

- As with real-world personas, your online persona should also be respectful, professional and courteous – make sure any public posts, pictures and videos convey the same impression.
- Unsure of how you're being presented? Google yourself to get a sense of what recruiters, employers, colleagues and prospective customers or coworkers are seeing – and take action accordingly.
- Use a polite, professional tone and considerate demeanor, as well as proper spelling and grammar, while communicating online, even when engaging in personal exchanges – all may be visible to the public at large, and influence their perception of you.
- Embarrassing and unflattering photos or videos should not be captured or publicly shared, as they may present unwelcome and unrepresentative images of your character to observers.
- More employers and job recruiters are turning to Google, Bing and other online search engines to research prospective hires – be aware of the image you're presenting to the world, and how it may be perceived.
- Configure social network settings so that personal information is kept private, and separate from work-related activity.
- Make sure your online portfolio, links to work examples and your résumé are truthful, factually representative and sparkle.
- Ensure your online brand reflects the same professionalism, personality and talent you show in real life. Be yourself, no matter what world you operate in, and be the same you that you are in any public situation.
- Seek out ways to establish thought leadership and goodwill, and to give back to the larger online community – making a positive impact is both personally rewarding and helps you generate a positive impression.
- If you have a website designed for professional purposes, make sure all content contained within it is appropriately professional in nature.
- All online presences – even on social networks such as Facebook, LinkedIn and

Twitter – should match the persona you project in real-life, and be consistent across platforms.

## Using Social Media to Hunt for Jobs

• Make sure all online profiles, e.g. your presence on LinkedIn, are up to date, current and engaging to potential employers.

• Sometimes, the most immediate way to learn of new job openings is to visit blogs, websites and follow tweets of those who could hire you on a daily basis. Be respectful of them and do not attempt to publicly solicit offers of employment, and follow any instructions posted with regard to submissions when positions are posted.

• If you are currently seeking work, it is appropriate to post a "Currently seeking new opportunities" status on LinkedIn, Facebook, Twitter or other social media channels to let others know. Be specific however: Tell what kind of position you're seeking, and how your experience applies (e.g. "Currently seeking new opportunities in the software development space – 10+ years of management of engineering experience.")

• Before you hit the send button with your résumé, research potential companies and managers via the Internet, as well as LinkedIn, Facebook,  Twitter and other channels. It pays to go in informed, and these channels can provide useful information about the people and businesses you are targeting for employment.

• You may wish to consider hyperlinking your résumé on LinkedIn and Twitter so that potential employers can find out about your skill set quickly and easily.

• Join online chats and discussions that relate to your area of expertise – especially if you can retweet, provide expertise to or help out people who might wish to hire you.

• While the virtual world can be a great way to get a jumpstart on job hunting, real-life follow-up is necessary, and online networking alone cannot serve as a total replacement for personal interactions – phone calls, meetings and business networking opportunities remain a key part of any holistic strategy.

## Stand Out Online in a Positive Way

• Creating content such as articles, videos and podcasts that showcases your expertise or helps others solve problems isn't just helpful and a great way to give back – it can also showcase your talents, help build your online reputation and create priceless goodwill.

• Extensive research should be undertaken before reaching out to potential employers or prospects – one size fits all pitches should typically be avoided in favored of personalized communiqués that show you've done your homework.

• If a company uses a specific tone of voice or terminology in press releases, tweets and on its website, you may wish to use similar words and phrasing when reaching out to hiring managers or when retweeting or connecting online.

- Thoroughly read job applications to make sure that you have followed given instructions, and that your skills and experience match the talents that the employer is seeking.
- Cover letters should be provided with all submissions and tailored to the specific employer – like follow-up communications, it should be clearly, concisely and respectfully written, and show that you've both done your homework, and can bring significant insight to the discussion.
- With regard to online applications, you may wish to follow submissions up with a call after a respectful timeframe to confirm that your résumé and application were received. Be polite, and if you have any specific questions about the job you applied for, ask respectfully, and you might get additional insight into the job or company that can help you. If no response is forthcoming to your queries after a reasonable number of tries to reach the other party – e.g. two attempts – it may be wisest to cease attempting communication.

**How to Follow, But Not Stalk Potential Employers**
- Do follow, friend, link, like and search online to find out more about potential companies and their hiring managers.
- Be polite and always follow up on both communications outreach or requests made by prospective employers in a timely manner.
- If employees of the corporation you wish to work for engage in social media exchanges, do consider engaging with them politely by retweeting relevant information, sharing pertinent data or responding to queries posted – just make sure you do so in a professional fashion.
- Engaging in conversation with potential employers online is acceptable, but don't be rude, obnoxious or overbearing in your online exchanges, or transparent or relentless about your intentions.
- It's OK to make polite inquiries about job openings, share your résumé, or link to your online portfolio if you can do so in a positive way that organically fits into a conversation. As in real life, you should never be too pushy or forward.
- Always present yourself in a respectful, authoritative and professional manner when dealing with businesses and brands online, just as you would with individual people.

## PERSONAL BRANDING AND SOCIAL MEDIA

Dan Schawbel, owner of Millennial Branding (www.MillenialBranding.com) and author of Me 2.0 is one of today's top experts on personal branding. We asked him to share his tips on how to better build your personal brand without breaching rules of etiquette through online, social and new media channels.

**Q:** One of the most common mistakes professionals make when it comes to personal branding is being shamelessly self-aggrandizing. How can you promote yourself without bragging?

**A:** You have to walk a fine line, right? A lot of people over-promote themselves, thinking that it's all about them. They're not using online vehicles to share valuable information that relates to their expertise, so what ends up happening is that no-one wants to follow them.   In order to build up any rep, be it on Facebook or through online marketing channels, it comes down to offering something that's useful to people and helps solve their problems. Once you stop doing that and it becomes all about you, people tune out—and the online world makes it very easy to opt out. It only takes one click. It's important to always give more value than you take. When you help out other people without asking for anything, then they'll probably want to help you out in return.

**Q:** How do you help create value for other people without being annoying or overbearing?

**A:** The way I see it, you should pick something, and it should become your focus point. Become the curator for that one niche. I don't think "enough" is "too much." People are not going to look down on you. Obviously, if you tweet a thousand times a day people are going to unfollow you, but you're still going to lose some followers that are just not as interested in your topic as you think they would be.

**Q:** So in regards to social media, influencers play the role of curators. But what other roles do you need to play to represent yourself? Do you need to be an opinionated commenter? Should you be a content creator? Is it a mix of all of the above?

**A:** You have to decide how you want to present yourself online. The people who voice their opinion on subject matter and don't just retweet certain topics about the subject matter are going to win out more because you don't want to appear as a robot. Once you do that, you become unique. There could be a thousand people in your niche who are all just retweeting the same article, but if you share that article and add commentary, then it's something very different.

**Q:** With regards to that, what are some of the rules of etiquette that have to be observed when you're talking about personal branding online?

**A:** Unless you want to focus on race, politics, class, or gender for some reason, typically you should stay away from those types of hot-button topics. They tend to isolate people. Focus on something you're really interested in—something you'll dedicate years to, but also where there's room to grow and there's not as much competition. Create your own world. Personal branding wasn't something that was talked about until social networking took off. Almost everything has been done before, but you need to take your own slant to it. You need your own angle.

**Q:** What do professionals need to know about reaching out via social media?

**A:** It takes time. Brands are not built overnight – doing so is a long-term process. Your brand needs to be cultivated over weeks, months, years. You need to start small and work yourself up. Follow certain people. Retweet them. Ask questions, answer some of the things they're saying, share resources so that people get to see your name and your face. Then when you email them or add them on Facebook, the probability that they'll accept you is much greater, because they're familiar with you. It's one of the reasons you should write articles for trade magazines, blog, speak, and get your name out there. You'll get more of your emails answered because people are familiar with who you are. "Personal branding" is less about your personal brand and more about people coming to you because they already know you, and they already know what you can do.

**Q:** Is it okay to contact someone blind via LinkedIn and reach out with a request right away?

**A:** I've done everything [in business outreach]. It's hard for me to say "Don't do that" because I have done that. You need to do whatever you think is right at the time, and you have to pay attention to who you're talking to. If you're talking to an executive, you might have to be smarter about how you phrase things. It depends on what your goals are, too. Are you a job seeker? Are you looking to get a new client? You have to judge each situation differently.

When the media reaches out to me on a topic, if I have knowledge on that topic, I'll connect with them, and then they'll know about me and what I can provide. Next time they're writing something on that topic, they'll think of me. The other thing is sometimes reporters look for examples that they can use in their stories, and I'll tweet out "Looking for these types of people," and then I'll help them with their stories. That's another way to evolve the relationship, too.

If I'm pitching an HR executive, I'll either email them directly and make it clear about what the relationship would look like, or I'll do these big media campaigns and a percentage of people will come to the website and fill out our forms and download eBooks. Then I'll contact them after that process.

As for the most effective way of reaching out, people are most receptive to email, but you have to do everything, especially if you're in business. See what works, do more of what works, test things out. You just have to fight for it.

**Q:** Is there any advice you'd give to professionals using personal branding that can help make them stand out without going too far over the top?

**A:** I think what's important is that you be your own brand management advisor. You need to think about different ways you're coming off to end users. You need to listen to feedback, and overall, you want to be yourself. That's really important. A lot of people brand themselves a certain way online, then when you meet them offline, they're so indifferent. That ruins the experience because it's not consistent, and then people kind of feel ripped off. It's important to be yourself, but also manage things as well. When I go on Facebook, I don't immediately post; I think twice before I do it. I check to make sure that what I'm posting is good, and that I think it'll do well, and it won't paint me in a negative light. I try to inspire young people, so I want to make sure that message is coming out. I don't want to subtract from that.

**Q:** What advice you might give bloggers, website owners, and forum posters about how they can be more effective about story creation or comments. A lot of people have a blog—how do you attract an audience without being an attention hog?

**A:** First, start getting your own content out there. Then keep on being consistent with that type of content, and go to the exact places where your audience is. Go to LinkedIn groups, go to forums, go anywhere they are and start commenting on the posts that they have. Instead of overloading yourself when you comment, just add some value or unique perspective. And when you comment on a blog, you usually get a link back to your site. When I first started out, I commented on any blog that mentioned personal branding. That's how people started to know me, especially in that community, which established the early relationships that propelled my brand forward. It's important to support what everyone else is doing and promote their work, and then hopefully a portion will help you back.

**Q:** What key piece of advice would you most give job seekers or professionals when it comes to personal branding?

**A:** I think people really need to focus on defining their brand. A lot of people get out there and start doing a mash-up of different things. That's not a good way of going about it because you can't be everything to everyone. Just really define what it is you're trying to do, and what audience you're trying to serve. If you get crystal-clear on that, then you have a better chance of really managing your brand. The tools are never as important as how you're going to present yourself, so once you figure that out, you just blend that across all the social networks, and it's consistent, and people know what you're about. But also keep in the back of your head that things change, and you need to evolve. I changed my whole business this year, so you have to be willing to change and adapt. That's how you survive.

# INTERNET AND ONLINE SAFETY

As modern technology users, we're eager to take to the cloud, using the Internet to reach new customers, touch base with existing clients and, in effect, communicate with the world. But the ease of using the Internet belies its risks. Millions of us share our business news on Facebook, with several million using check-in services like Foursquare and Path to tell people our every move. Meanwhile, we're replacing old-fashioned hard drives with cloud-based storage solutions like those provided by Apple, Google, Dropbox, Carbonite and Hightail, putting our precious, valuable, and, in some cases, even intimate information into virtual vaults for safekeeping. But, old-fashioned security shouldn't be replaced completely by virtual vaults, especially when it comes to sensitive and important corporate information. It's worth noting that Facebook, Path, and Dropbox have all suffered major security breaches, reminding us how insecure our secure information really could be at any given moment.

Mobile security is crucial to keep in mind, too. According to Javelin Research, nearly one out of every ten smartphone owners has been a victim of identity theft in recent years. This was likely because a third of smartphone users didn't update to the latest, most secure software and a whopping two-thirds had no password installed on their phone – even when their phone was their primary link to the office! Today's cell phones are more powerful than yesterday's computers, and yet we don't always remember the power we have in our hands – and the potential authority that we place in someone else's if these devices are stolen.

Interacting wisely online and being a responsible digital employer or employee is the last piece to understanding holistic Internet security. In this day and age, appropriate online etiquette and conduct not only refers to maintaining proper manners, but being smart with how you protect yourself and your business online as well.

## General Tips

### Adding Antivirus and Pop-Up Blockers

• It is a myth that smartphones and Mac computers do not get viruses, so make sure that all your mobile devices and systems have the latest anti-virus and anti-spam protection software installed. Many companies offer paid solutions (following free 30-day trials), while others provide completely free alternatives.

• Regularly update programs and operating systems. Take software update notices seriously as they may patch up a security breach in your current software, device or operating system's settings.

- Nearly every modern Web browser has a built-in pop-up blocker to stop spam ads, often found under the Preferences menu.

**Preventing Identity Theft and Data Breaches**

- Create secure passwords that employ a sequence of numbers, letters, and characters into a code that only you know.
- Do not use the same password on multiple sites.
- If you need to keep a record of your passwords on your PC (not advised), be sure to encrypt the file.
- Avoid odd or unexpected email attachments, as they may contain spam or harmful programs, and have senders give you a heads-up before they send attachments or add-ons.
- Cloud backup solutions are convenient, but be aware that anything uploaded to the Internet may be fair game for third-parties to access should a security breach occur – consider the sensitivity of the data you store remotely.
- Make sure that all software is completely up to date and your virus protection subscription is current.
- If an incoming call or email seems suspicious, hang up or close the email and contact the company directly through the main number or email contained on their official website or other corporate channels. Do not click on any links in suspicious emails, or use phone numbers contained within.

**Protecting Yourself from Criminals and Predators**

- Assume any opportunities to make money quickly (i.e. get rich quick schemes) are traps. Chances are, you probably don't know an exiled Nigerian prince, or have a rich uncle who's just dying to hand over $1 million.
- Make it a policy to change your online passwords at least once a month, and more frequently if you perform a lot of online transactions.
- If you call for assistance with a website, the Help Center will rarely, if ever ask for your online password or full personal details – the last four digits of a credit card are more likely. If you're worried of putting your personal credit card at risk, consider using prepaid cards for any online activity.
- Look for odd word choices, suspicious behavior, and other telltale signs of fraudulent activity when you're interacting with a new face online, and consider any oddities shown or strange requests made during conversation.
- Do not connect with strangers through social networks, as it exposes any

information shared on them, potentially including valuable details of your everyday life, to someone you don't know.

## What Not to Share Online

• Never share information online that you wouldn't give to a stranger, including phone numbers, social security numbers, addresses, hometowns, birthdays and other personal details.

• Use caution with location-based mobile software, including social networks, photo sharing and search apps, which can tell strangers where you are if you don't restrict their privacy settings.

• Many new apps allow you to use your Facebook, Twitter, Google+ or LinkedIn account to log in, but, if possible, create a separate username/password rather than linking them to core accounts and sharing your private user information.

• Do not share your social security number online or, if you absolutely must (e.g. in the case of interactions with the government), always provide it to a trusted, live representative over a secure connection where possible rather than over email or via a website.

• Before giving out your billing information and address, make sure you're using a website that provides a secure connection by looking for the word "Secure" or a lock symbol in the corner of your web browser.

• Accurate ages, names and birthdates are required for flights and similarly sensitive or government-regulated services. But in the case of services where they're not legally required, consider opting out or entering false information to avoid needlessly handing out precious personal information.

• Most companies do not need your phone number when registering for services, as often your email address will suffice. Always opt out of providing personal information if it isn't required.

• If you want to get off an email list, nearly every company has a link at the bottom of its newsletter titled "Unsubscribe" that will remove you from mailings.

"Being cognizant of the type of websites you're visiting is the first step to staying safe online. Don't access sites that require you compromise confidential information, like online banking accounts, credit card numbers, etc., and never do so from public computers and WiFi networks. Visit secure websites, always log-off of sites and close out of them when you're done using them."

-Jeana Lee Tahnk, www.jeanatahnk.com, Tech Writer and PR Consultant

### How to Share Your Email Address Without Being Spammed

• When applying for contests or other promotions that require plugging information into online entry forms, consider creating a "dummy" email address through one of the free email providers.

• If you do receive a company email requesting that you confirm your password, go directly to the company's official website and login to do it securely rather than clicking on a link in the original email.

• If an email looks suspicious, do an online search to see if there are any recent scams related to the company emailing you.

### The Ethics of Employers Asking for Your Online Passwords

• You are not legally required to give your employer passwords to your social networks or personal sites.

• Be careful befriending or connecting with co-workers or supervisors online, as they will be able to access personal thoughts, information, and items shared (or that others have posted about you or on your profile) through your online connection without needing to ask for passwords.

• Should you choose to share your password, ask them to notify you as soon as they're finished utilizing them, and change passwords immediately upon notification. Always change your password immediately after leaving their employment.

### Safely Visiting Personal Sites at Work and Vice Versa

• Monitoring and tracking systems are standard for work computers, so use extreme caution when visiting personal, social, leisure or questionable sites while at work.

• Understand that your employer could use your email and web browsing habits (all of which they may be able to legally access and track) at work against you.

• Log out of any personal websites whenever you step away from your work computer, including during lunch and coffee breaks.

• Before you work from home or on a public computer, ask your company if there is any security protocol you need to follow.

• Be aware that any information shared or exchanged over public WiFi networks (such as those available at hotels, airports and coffee shops) may be visible to others.

### Ways to Secure Work Computers and Mobile Devices

• Password protect all accounts, software programs and network account logins with unique and not easily guessable (birthdates, anniversaries, etc.) passcodes. Do not share your password with anyone.

• Log out of all personal websites, apps and software programs when finished using them, and close and secure all work-related documents, programs and websites when you are done working.

- Use password-protected flash drives, hard drives or secure online services to minimize the transfer of sensitive work-related data between work and personal emails. Do not share sensitive data over instant messengers or other solutions that may be subject to security breach. Be advised that anything uploaded to the Internet may potentially be shared and access by others.
- Secure any work-related computers and mobile devices with a password only known by you. Use a combination of letters, numbers and characters, and not one related to common dictionary terms, for stronger password protection.
- Pre-install remote-wiping software to remove any sensitive information when a device is lost or stolen. You may also wish to do the same with device tracking and protection software, which allows you to locate and lock missing devices, sound built-in alarms or shut down devices remotely.
- Shut down computers and devices when not in use.
- Do not leave sensitive documents or data lying out on your desk – especially overnight.

# INSTANT MESSAGING AND CHAT ROOMS

Instant messenger (IM) programs provide an easy and convenient way to conduct conversations with others including colleagues and clients quickly, and not just enjoy a personal LOL (laugh out loud) with friends. Skype, MSN Messenger, Yahoo!'s chat solutions and a variety of other instant messaging services and tools are all very adaptable for business uses as well as personal use. Instead of conducting a conference call with a supplier in South America, you can Skype, for example; similarly, you can also give a speech to a remote auditorium using Google+'s Hangouts videoconferencing feature. Though instant messaging has lost some steam in recent years, given the rise of social networks and texting options, the practice still has its place for brief, direct and private conversations, and using it correctly can help businesses operate more smoothly.

Instant messaging usually consists of one-on-one dialogue in the form of text updates between individuals, but in any circumstances – solo or shared – basic rules of social etiquette still apply. Treat conversations made over instant messenger solutions as sincerely and as carefully as you would a face-to-face chat. As such, proper business etiquette always applies.

## General Tips

- When choosing a screen name, select one that's professional, polite and appropriate for viewing in shared company. Be aware that alternating capitals, abbreviations, and combinations of mixed numbers and letters may be perceived as less suitable than simple aliases (e.g. JohnQPublic instead of JqPDude1401). This can be especially true, depending on your business.
- Keep interactions with others polite, respectful and professional, and be aware that others may see your communications.
- Do not share sensitive information via an instant messenger, even with trusted associates, as a slip of a finger or security breach could easily expose this data.
- Be cognizant of others' time: Consider whether repeated messages may interrupt and annoy them as they work or go about their business.
- Set your status to Away or Do Not Disturb if you do not wish to be interrupted by incoming messages.
- Remember to change your status when you step away from your device and return, especially since you don't want to give the impression that you're ignoring someone's requests, or take multi-hour lunch breaks.

- Respect people's current IM status: Leave them alone if it says Busy, stop contacting them if it says In a Meeting, and so forth.
- Note that while others' statuses may indicate that they are available, they may not be, having inadvertently stepped away from their device, or become preoccupied with an important work-related task. Do not spam them with messages if you don't get an immediate response.
- Do not send instant messages while engaged in phone or real-world conversations. It is OK, however, to send an occasional IM if directly related to the dialogue – e.g. messaging a colleague to help answer a pressing IT question the person on the phone has presented.
- When exiting or pausing a conversation, be polite and drop a note to the other party to let them know ("have to run – see you later!").
- Use caution when conducting multiple conversations, as typing a response intended for another party, or erroneously cutting and pasting links or snippets of conversation into the wrong window, could cause serious trouble and confusion.

## Avoiding Potential Misunderstandings Over IM
- Like email, IM is usually too limited to have complex, nuanced conversations – save subtleties for direct, more personal forms of communication
- If asking a deep or serious question, give the recipient adequate time to reply before you talk again.
- Keep in mind that most IM programs tell the recipient when the other person is typing, so don't interrupt the recipient by typing while they are typing their own response.

## Appropriately Conducting Multiple Conversations
- Briefly overlapping conversations are OK, but you should excuse yourself from one of the conversations if both continue beyond a few responses.
- It is totally acceptable to tell one recipient Be Right Back, or brb, if you need to step away from the device, or are wrapping up a second conversation.
- People speaking to you in person should take priority over the people on IM. Under no circumstance should direct personal contact or conversations be ignored in favor of instant messenger prompts – be polite when spoken to and give those present in real-life your full and undivided attention.

## When Instant Messaging is Appropriate at Work
- Consider your work environment, as IM is much more appropriate in a 400-person building than a three-person office.
- Given its potential to alternately distract or facilitate faster communication in certain

cases, be advised that employer policies on IM may widely differ. Determine which policies and rules of conduct apply to your workplace by talking with your supervisor or, if you are in charge, deciding what potential effect the introduction of IM would have on employees and the daily workflow.

• Note that employers may reserve the right to track, monitor and review any IM conversations made on the job.

## What IM Subjects are Safe for the Workplace

• Minor details on current projects and small questions relevant to your current job or task at-hand are suitable for asking over IM. More important, sensitive or detailed questions should be made via email, in-person meetings or direct phone call.

• Work IM should not be used for jokes, questionable material, or other items not related to your job.

• Be cautious using instant messaging when contacting neighboring co-workers, as communications made this way are impersonal enough that they may get the impression that you don't want to talk to them for some reason.

## Addressing Perceived Harassment Over IM

• If you believe that you are being harassed, set your IM program so that it records conversations and provide documented archives to your HR department or direct supervisor.

• Consider blocking the harassing person on IM.

• Create clear boundaries on IM by only discussing topics relevant to work.

## When to Shut Instant Messengers Off

• Always set your IM program to Busy, Do Not Disturb or, better yet, shut it down entirely while conducting meetings in your office or speaking on the phone.

• When around others, keep your IM program's sound effects and audio notifications settings turned off unless you're using headphones.

• Turn off instant messaging programs whenever you leave the office for the day, even if office policy is to leave your computers on all night.

# CONCLUSION

There are few, if any, times in human history where technology has played such an important and overarching role in our everyday lives. Today, we're more mobile than ever, with companies suddenly selling more smartphones than PCs, and lightning-fast Internet service now available even to the most remote third world countries. Society and business have become more connected than ever before, with Facebook boasting nearly a billion users and corporate change already being affected with a single tweet. In short, we have to learn how to better respect our colleagues and our clients, and be cognizant of how our actions impact them, within this new world order.

Many of the strategies advocated here, however, can be distilled into five basic, easily remembered points:

- Don't share personal information. Clearly separate the personal from the professional world.
- Save important conversations for face-to-face talks.
- Think before you post, and consider how others will perceive what you share.
- Be fully present when you connect with others in real life.
- Conduct yourself with utmost professionalism.

The irony: In reality, business netiquette is really much the same as traditional etiquette – technology has simply become so intertwined in our everyday business that the courtesy, thoughtfulness, and priorities we value in person now must be applied to our virtual operations as well.

Now it's your turn. Apply the ideas, guidelines, and perspectives given here in your own career and business. Talk with others about how technology is changing your job, and how we as professionals and digital citizens can be smarter and more responsible about integrating the best it has to offer within our day-to-day routines. Finally, recognize that rules of online and high-tech etiquette will only continue to evolve alongside the ever-growing torrent of apps, gadgets and online services. Only through continued conversation, and the participation of all sides involved, can we hope to stay ahead of the curve.

We'd be honored if you'd join us and share your discoveries, with an eye towards shaping future editions of the guide, and providing a roadmap for tomorrow's digital employers and employees. We invite you to reach out and join the conversation at www.AKeynoteSpeaker.com.

In the meantime, remember that technology can be fun, inspiring, and even life-changing when treated with proper dignity and respect, and as part of a well-balanced media diet. We sincerely hope that you've found this guide to be a helpful resource — and the first small step in a journey to become a better, brighter and more positive contributor to tomorrow's high-tech world.

# ADDITIONAL HINTS AND TIPS

## Rich DeMuro (@RichDeMuro), Tech Reporter, KTLA-TV Los Angeles

**Q:** The most common breaches of high-tech etiquette you see people making and potential solutions to these problems would be?

**A:** The most common issues I see are people breaking the no texting or hands on phone talking while driving rules many states have set up. Not only is it really dangerous to do these things, but if I can't do it, then why should you be able to? Remember — 99.9% of emails and texts can wait.

Also, for some reason, people are still commonly sending forwards that contain false information. Before you send any "good to know" email to a bunch of people, do a quick fact check on Snopes.com. Most of the time, your email's information was debunked years ago.

**Q:** Any advice for friending new people on Facebook?

**A:** If you're going to friend someone on Facebook, make sure you know them first! If it's someone you just met and you think you'll become friends, wait a bit before you actually friend them on Facebook unless you're certain the feeling is mutual. Everyone uses social networks differently (e.g. some for work, some for personal reasons), so try to get a feel for someone before you friend them. If they have a friends list that numbers in the thousands, they probably don't mind the random friend request. If it's in the low hundreds, they probably closely guard who they let into their circle. If it's a business thing, include a note with your request so they have a frame of reference to remember who you are.

**Q:** How do you de-friend someone on Facebook without causing a stir?

**A:** De-friending people on Facebook is a very touchy subject. No one wants to be de-friended. Even if you never talk to that person in real life, it just feels sad to get cut. Think about it this way — there must have been some reason why you friended the person in the first place. Instead of de-friending, consider adding them to Facebook's "Restricted" friends list. They will no longer be able to see much of your wall or profile and won't get any more updates from you. Then unsubscribe from their updates so you don't have to see their mugshot in your news feed. That way, it's almost like you're no longer friends but you technically still are.

**Q:** When is it OK to use a high-tech device (phones, etc.) in public? When should one absolutely be shut off?

**A:** At this point, it's becoming pretty commonplace to see gadgets just about everywhere. Our phones are our cameras and our cameras are our phones, which has opened up an entire world of possibilities. At this point, I'd go with the flow. If you see people using their devices, feel free. If there is a sign saying no phones, respect it. Otherwise, definitely keep them silent and in your pocket during meetings and important real-life conversations.

**Q:** How should you comport yourself on messaging services and text-based networks like Twitter? Any ways to avoid making huge social mistakes?

**A:** Twitter is a mixed bag. The good news about Twitter is that it's either public or private. There is no in-between, which frees you up when you're posting. You know your potential audience is the world. My advice is to keep your audience in mind — figure out who is following you and why, and deliver what they would expect to see from you. Everyone uses Twitter differently, so establish why you're on there and just do it.

**Q:** Any top tips you can share for being a better digital citizen?

**A:** Everyone uses the web in different ways and there is a place for everything. My best advice is to think before you do just about anything. Do you really need to make that call while eating a burger in the car? Does anyone care about your 99th check-in at Starbucks? I'm not saying don't do it, but not everything has to be shared with everyone. Otherwise, just realize your strengths — be it witty commentator, early adopter or curator of cute photos — and go with it.

## Christina Tynan-Wood, Author of Family Circle's Family Tech column and How to Be a Geek Goddess

**Q:** Essential rules as relate to modern-day high-tech, online and social networking manners include?

**A:** I don't really have any hard and fast rules that are different for social networking than they are for real life. If it's rude in person, it's rude online. I like manners. They were created for good reason: To help people sharing space get along better. This is why you see cultures with the smallest amount of space caring the most about manners. And I was raised by a well-mannered English woman. But I think the Internet reflects a lot of cultures, which is why it is so easy to offend. Everyone has their own idea of well-mannered.

For me, too much information is rude. So I'm offended when people share photos of intimate parts, surgeries, gross flesh wounds, etc. But some people are fascinated by this sort of thing, or there would be no reality TV. I don't think it's my business to tell other people what they should do online. But I do quietly un-friend people who share too much.

Note that un-friending is easy and best done quietly. Facebook doesn't tell people you have un-friended them so all you have to do is click that little X to get rid of them. If they are associates who will notice they have been un-friended, I hide them instead.

As for friending, I like to know who I'm friending because letting people into my Facebook page gives them access to my other friends and that includes my children. But other people have their own rules about this either because they like to meet perfect strangers and are willing to take risks to do it or because they are using social media to promote a business.

**Q:** Your number one no-no when it comes to how users behave on social networks?

**A:** I don't like to tell people what to do as far as comporting yourself. In fact, I tend to silence or un-friend people who are strident and bossy online. There are a lot of different reasons for using social media and different rules apply to each. If you are just starting out at this, though, it's a good idea to stick to the basic rule (so as not to embarrass yourself): If you wouldn't stand up in front of a crowd and shout it, don't say it on Facebook or Twitter. Though some people clam up completely in front of a crowd so that rule won't really work for them.

**Q:** How about using high-tech devices in public – any tips you can offer there?

**A:** When it comes to using devices in public places, I'm pretty liberal. They are a great way to entertain yourself while alone in restaurants. Sometimes you really do have to take that call. But if you are socializing with people and talking to someone else on the phone, you know you are being rude. But being rude by accident or because you are a phone addict will cost you real-world friends, clients or associates.

The only real "Do Not Do It!" I have (assuming you are an intelligent person capable of managing your own relationships or going without them if that is the natural consequence of your own actions) is DO NOT TEXT WHILE DRIVING. Harming your friends, passengers, and complete strangers on the road because you can't control your impulses is completely unacceptable behavior in every culture.

## Michael Dsupin, CEO, Talener Group

**Q:** A couple suggestions for appropriate blog commenting would include...?

Blog authors love comments. It validates their message or it validates that they are blogging about a point near to readers' hearts — whether you agree or disagree is irrelevant.  The fact that their post hit a nerve and you chose to share your feedback matters most.

When leaving a comment, the commentator is trying to engage the author. Here are a few quick tips to make sure your blog comments are most meaningful:

- First, make sure that you use firsthand experiences and real examples to support your opinion, either pro or con.
- Second, try to be as brief as possible, yet as thorough as possible.
- Third, comment on a blog post ASAP for maximum coverage and engagement.
- Fourth, make sure you use your full name, title and company that you work for, so people can Google you and read more about your background to determine your credibility level. Take for instance a restaurant recommendation that might read, "Mike says that the calamari is excellent." It's better to read that "Mike is really Mike Smith, executive chef at Per Se — thus making it a credible recommendation.

**Q:** When is it most appropriate to attempt to make a connection on LinkedIn?

**A:** Connecting with people on LinkedIn is nice to do, but not a required business practice.  Therefore, I would not stop my current prospecting or business development to send an immediate LinkedIn request. I would recommend waiting until the next break, lunch or end of the day to send the request. You don't want to look too aggressive or desperate, but you do want to be timely. Don't use LinkedIn requests as a way to try to engage someone who knows that you are waiting for a response on a certain matter.

**Q:** What is the most common social gaffe people make with their cell phone?

**A:** The most social gaffe is sending an email or text before it was completed. I have hit send prematurely on countless occasions and I hate that feeling. Another one is closing lines on signatures that ask, "Please ignore any typos or spelling mistakes." Really? Do we have to ask for forgiveness? Come on man!

## Judith Kallos, Creator, NetManners.com

**Q:** What should you do if you boss wants to be friends on Facebook?

**A:** Politely let them know that you appreciate your personal privacy being respected and that you do not "friend" those who you have a strictly professional relationship with. Now, if you are really friends in the true sense of the word, you wouldn't ask that question, right?

**Q:** Is it appropriate to automatically follow people on Twitter?

**A:** Not unless you are truly interested in what they have to say....

**Q:** Is there an appropriate way to respect them and not follow them back?

**A:** Following has nothing to do with respect. Because someone you don't know (or even possibly do) follows you does not mean that you have an obligation to follow them back. It's the same with friending. Chances are they won't even notice if you do or not anyway.

## Tim Stevens, Editor-in-Chief, Engadget

**Q:** What is the most common social flub that people make when it comes to using mobile devices and cell phones?

**A:** Far and away the most common social gaffe people make with their phones is pulling them out in the middle of small social gatherings, say, dinner out with a colleague. This is definitely increasing in terms of social acceptance, but it's still rude to whip out your smartphone while someone is talking to you. It's always best to wait for them to take their phone out first or, if you must peek, at least wait for the conversation to die down.

Far less common but far more annoying is a phone ringing during a movie. There's a reason that the pre-show trailers remind you three times to silence your phones. Don't be that guy or gal who needs a fourth reminder!

**Q:** Is there an elegant, unobtrusive way to get rid of unwanted Facebook friends?

**A:** There is no really easy and graceful way to do it, unfortunately. A lot of people post an update saying "Sorry, I need to prune my friends list, it's nothing personal." But that's just the equivalent of saying that "I have friends I like more than you." The best you can do is move someone to a list that sees none of your status updates and has limited access to your info on there. That way you're still "friends" but they aren't seeing your every move.

**Q:** How can people be more productive commenters on blogs, newsgroups and other public forums?

**A:** The best way to be a good commenter is to relax! People get incredibly uptight, defensive and offensive. Nobody likes a troll, even other trolls, and if you find yourself getting into fights in comments sections constantly, chances are you need to get out from under that bridge!

# ABOUT SCOTT STEINBERG

Bestselling business author Scott Steinberg is one of the world's most celebrated professional speakers, futurists, and strategic innovation consultants, as seen in 600+ outlets from CNN to The Wall St. Journal. The CEO of management consulting and market research firm TechSavvy Global, he helps clients create value and cultivate competitive advantage on the back of emerging innovations and trends. A top-rated provider of keynote speeches, workshops and seminars for Fortune 500 businesses, non-profits, associations and educational institutes, he's partnered with many leading organizations to deliver game-changing leadership, education, and change management programs. As a trusted advisor to the world's biggest and most well-known brands, he's consulted on dozens of innovative products, services, and marketing and social media campaigns.

Among today's most-quoted keynote speakers and trend experts, as seen by over one billion people worldwide, Scott's 10+ year track record for accurately predicting business, consumer and technology trends has made him a fixture in mainstream media. Today's #1-ranked technology expert according to Google, he's been a syndicated columnist on change and innovation for numerous outlets ranging from Fast Company, Inc. and Entrepreneur to Rolling Stone and The Huffington Post. An acclaimed entrepreneur who's built and sold several startups and divisions, recent works include Becoming Essential, The Crowdfunding Bible, Teaching Technology and the award-winning Business Expert's Guidebook. His motivational speeches, leadership seminars and training workshops are renowned for demonstrating thousands how to become more successful and effective in their life and career.

For more, see **www.AKeynoteSpeaker.com.**

"One of the best gurus on innovation and competitive advantage strategies to accelerate growth."
--European Commission

"If you really want to know about business, you should refer to Scott Steinberg."
--Sir Richard Branson, Virgin Group

## Popular Speeches Include

-- Leading with Innovation: How to Future-Proof Yourself + Succeed Going Forward

-- Change Management: Creating a Culture of Innovation

-- Becoming Essential: How to Build & Maintain Competitive Advantage

-- The New Rules of Marketing, PR and Social Media

-- The Relationship Economy - Reinventing Sales and Customer Service

-- Seeing Tomorrow Today: How to Stay Ahead of the Curve

# ADDITIONAL RESOURCES

For more helpful resources, including free eBooks, tip sheets, training guides and videos, please visit us online at **www.AKeynoteSpeaker.com**.

Additional books and training guides by Scott Steinberg include:

- BECOMING ESSENTIAL: BUILDING GROWTH, VALUE AND COMPETITIVE ADVANTAGE THROUGH STRATEGIC INNOVATION

- SOCIAL MEDIA MARKETING AND MANAGEMENT

- CONTENT MARKETING: THE INSIDER SECRETS

- INFLUENCER MARKETING

- CUSTOMER SERVICE IS BROKEN

- PROFESSIONAL SPEAKERS, MEETINGS AND EVENTS MADE SIMPLE

- CROWDFUNDING AND KICKSTARTER: THE ULTIMATE GUIDE

- THE BUSINESS EXPERT'S GUIDEBOOK - #1 Bestseller

- THE CROWDFUNDING BIBLE - #1 Bestseller

- THE MODERN PARENT'S GUIDE: HIGH-TECH PARENTING - #1 Bestseller

- FACEBOOK FOR KIDS AND PARENTS - Bestseller

# DEDICATION

For Z and all those doing business with a more human
touch today.